DATE DUE

NOV 2 0 2013	
MAY 1 5 2015	
MAY 2 7 2015	
July 21, 2015	

BRODART, CO.   Cat. No. 23-221

HOW TO
Say ANYTHING
TO ANYONE

A GUIDE TO BUILDING
BUSINESS RELATIONSHIPS
THAT REALLY WORK

SHARI HARLEY

GREENLEAF
BOOK GROUP PRESS

Published by Greenleaf Book Group Press
Austin, Texas
www.gbgpress.com

Distributed by Greenleaf Book Group LLC

For ordering information or special discounts for bulk purchases, please contact Candid Culture at 700 N. Colorado Blvd., #410, Denver, CO 80206, 303.863.0948.

Design and composition by Molly Moore
Cover design by Molly Moore

Cataloging-in-Publication data

Publisher's Cataloging-In-Publication Data
(Prepared by The Donohue Group, Inc.)

Harley, Shari.
    How to say anything to anyone : a guide to building business relationships that really work / Shari Harley. -- 1st ed.
      p. ; cm.
    Issued also as an ebook.
    ISBN: 978-1-60832-409-5
    1. Interpersonal relations. 2. Success in business. 3. Communication in management. 4. Trust--Social aspects. I. Title.
HM1106 .H37 2013
302/.1
2012942417

Part of the Tree Neutral® program, which offsets the number of trees consumed in the production and printing of this book by taking proactive steps, such as planting trees in direct proportion to the number of trees used: www.treeneutral.com

TreeNeutral

Printed in the United States of America on acid-free paper

12 13 14 15 16 17   10 9 8 7 6 5 4 3 2 1

CONTENTS

THE CASE FOR **CANDOR**

C andor is widely misunderstood and sadly lacking in most personal and professional relationships. Perhaps you feel the word *candor* has a negative connotation, and thus you don't believe you can afford to try it. But have you ever considered how a lack of candor affects you, both in business and in the rest of your life? Take a look at these scenarios.

- ▶ Have you ever interviewed for a position but failed to receive the job offer, and you never figured out why?
- ▶ Has a longtime friend ever suddenly stopped calling, with no explanation?
- ▶ Have you ever had a great date, but never heard from that person again?

I'll bet you wondered what went wrong in all those situations. What should you do differently to get the job the next time? What happened to that friendship—was it something you said or did? Why no second date?

If you're like most of us, instead of calling to find out what really happened, you made assumptions.

Now consider your relationships with people you are paying to provide a service. If you sit too long in your doctor's waiting room, do you tell your doctor that you consider the delay disrespectful and a waste of your time? Or do you find a new doctor? If your accountant makes a mistake, do you give feedback about the error, or do you find a new accountant? If you receive poor service in a restaurant, do you let the manager know, or do you just stop eating there?

My hunch is that you've kept quiet every time.

The fact is we're all a bunch of wimps. Even our closest friends don't speak up about the things we do that disappoint them. They don't want to cause conflict, hurt our feelings, or damage the relationship. But when someone does not speak up, the relationship is damaged anyway. If the offending behavior continues, friends drift away and the relationship dies.

NO NEWS IS NOT NECESSARILY **GOOD NEWS**

The same is true of our bosses and coworkers. The people we work with are afraid to confront us directly as problems accumulate. So we end up being caught off guard in performance reviews and meetings. Have you ever had a performance appraisal in which the feedback was all news to you—bad news? You thought you'd had a great year. Obviously, your boss didn't agree. Instead of giving you ongoing feedback throughout the year, she waited twelve months to tell you that you weren't meeting her expectations.

How many meetings have you attended in which you really needed your coworkers' support, but they said nothing? How many "happy" employees suddenly left your organization because they had ongoing frustrations and dissatisfactions you never knew about? How did those encounters make you feel? Wouldn't it have been great if you could have eliminated those situations entirely or at least gained enough control to dramatically minimize their occurrence?

All these issues stem from a lack of candor in our relationships. Unfortunately, many people associate the word *candor* with bad news. We tell ourselves we're being kind to our friends and the people we work with by not being candid and giving direct feedback. But we're not being kind. We're being timid, passive, and unhelpful.

HUMAN BEINGS ARE **"WHY" MACHINES**

As human beings, we have a need to know and understand why things occur. When we don't know, we make up stuff, and the stories we create are never good. *"I'm not good-looking enough, and I'll always be single." "My boss doesn't like me, and I have no future here."*

You might be right. You might be wrong. But either way, you're just guessing. In the business world, guessing is inefficient. It renders you, dare I say, impotent. You need to know what people are saying behind your back, because what people think and say about you impacts your career more than any project you deliver or sale you make.

YOU **CAN'T** WRITE YOURSELF A BIGGER PAYCHECK

What *you* think, unfortunately, makes no difference in your career. The only thing that matters is the other person's perspective of reality. If you're bored at work and think you're ready to take on more responsibility but your boss thinks you don't show enough initiative or that you need to strengthen your skills, your opinion won't get you promoted. If you think you provide great customer service but your customers don't agree, you'll lose them.

Here's the challenge: Most of us have no idea how we come across to others or what our employers and colleagues think of our services. We don't know what people think because, for the most part, they don't tell us. Instead, they tell other people behind our backs. This is why we need to encourage people to be candid with us, even when it hurts to hear their feedback. Otherwise, we'll operate under false assumptions and make unnecessary, career-killing mistakes.

SETTING THE RECORD STRAIGHT ON CANDOR

Candor is not bad news, and a candid organizational culture is not necessarily about saying hard things. Instead, candor is asking more questions at the onset of relationships. Candor is stating expectations rather than expecting employees and vendors to read your mind. Candor is making a commitment to talk about things as they happen, not six months after the fact.

Don't guess what people want or what they think about your performance. Ask them. In candid cultures, coworkers, employers, and employees say what they need to say quickly and easily. They have created relationships in which all parties can speak openly without concern.

YOU CREATE YOUR CAREER

You can create effective and open business relationships with no nasty surprises, and doing that will give you more power and control over your results. After all, information is power, and power is control. When you know what people think and say about you, you have choices. When you understand the impact of your behavior and consciously choose your outcomes, you are in charge of your career.

In contrast, when you don't know what others are thinking and saying, you don't know the impact of their opinions. You're operating in default mode. Other people are in charge of your career and your life.

What if building powerful and effective business relationships was as simple as asking the right questions? This book presents a proven strategy for business success that is as bold as it is simple: Ask more. Assume less.®

My commitment to you is that if you use the tools and techniques outlined in the remainder of this book, you will be able to:

▸ Establish trust in all your relationships
▸ Set expectations with coworkers, direct supervisors, and clients and tell others what you need
▸ Have smoother working relationships
▸ Decrease silos and increase partnerships on teams and between departments

- Get and keep the right employees and manage employees with more ease
- Get the best work from employees
- Earn more opportunities and responsibility
- Reduce gossip and drama in your office
- Become more efficient and eliminate redundancies
- Take charge of your career and your future
- Increase your career and life satisfaction

You are in charge of your career success and satisfaction. If you don't know it already, this book will help you understand that much of your career satisfaction lies in the quality of your working relationships. The chapters that follow provide a commonsense, easy-to-follow methodology to create smoother and more open working relationships that will enable you to get more done in less time.

If you want to take charge of your career, invest time in your business relationships. Ask questions about what people need, want, and are expecting from you. It's that simple.

CHAPTER 1

HOW TO ESTABLISH
CANDID RELATIONSHIPS

D id you buy this book hoping for the secret formula that would reveal how to safely tell your boss he's a jerk? Or to learn how to tell "the lingerer" (you know, that person who stops by your desk to drop something off and thirty minutes later is still blabbing about her personal life) to go away? Well, you're in luck. Later in this book, I'll give you that formula. *But the formula is not what you're missing.*

There is an abundance of books on how to give feedback— *Difficult Conversations*; *Fierce Conversations*; *Crucial Conversations*; and *Dealing with Difficult People* are just a few of the titles that are out there. Many of you have read them, and most organizations offer training on how to get through difficult conversations and manage conflict. Yet most people say nothing when others frustrate them.

You can read all the books and attend all the training programs you want, and it will make little difference. It's not just technique that you're lacking.

And it's not necessarily that you don't know what to say. It's that you feel you can't say what you want to say. You haven't been given permission. Without receiving prior permission, you feel at risk to speak up—so you don't.

What you're lacking is an agreement. You would never buy a car or rent an apartment without a contract. But you have relationships without contracts all the time. Where is the agreement that defines how you will work with your coworkers or customers, and how they will work with you? What? You've never heard of such an idea? Well, that's exactly why you're reading this book.

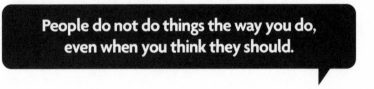

People do not do things the way you do, even when you think they should.

We assume people will do things the same way we do, such as be on time for appointments, pay their fair share in a restaurant, and tell us in advance if they're going to miss a deadline—because that's what we do. We don't tell people what we expect from them, because we don't think we need to.

It's a little like being frustrated that you weren't given a project to manage that you never asked for. Or hoping for a new iPad for your birthday but not telling anyone, and then being annoyed when you receive a series of coffee-table books that will go straight to your re-gifting shelf.

> **YOU:** "How could he not know I wanted an iPad?"
>
> **THE VOICE OF REASON:** "Because you never told him."
>
> **YOU:** "But I shouldn't have to tell him. He should just know."
>
> **THE VOICE OF REASON:** "Expecting people to know what you want without telling them is insane. How about this: Make a list of birthday gifts you want and ask permission to give the list to your significant other. Chances are he'll be relieved, and you may actually get what you want next year."

Here's a crazy idea: What if you started every relationship by creating an agreement about how you will treat each other?

TEACH PEOPLE HOW TO **WIN** WITH YOU

What if you set the expectation that when someone violates such an agreement—and it's only a matter of time before one of you does—you both not only have the right but are expected to say something?

Then people might just tell each other the truth.

For example, what if when you scheduled an appointment with a vendor who is notoriously late, you told her that promptness is important to you? You tell the vendor that you're looking forward to the meeting, but if she is more than fifteen minutes late, you're going to leave.

Having laid out this expectation, you might feel more justified in walking out at 12:20 when she still hasn't arrived for your twelve o'clock appointment than you would have if you had not set an expectation during your initial conversation.

For those of you who are thinking, *"That may happen to you, but it never happens to me. I would never allow it,"* here's another example. Have you ever had lunch with a friend or coworker who repeatedly stiffs you for part of the bill? Every time you go out he pays only for his $10.00 burger, *forgetting* to include tax and tip. Has that person shorted the bill more than once? Did you ever say anything? I'm guessing that instead of speaking up, you begrudgingly threw in a couple of extra dollars, while wondering why you continue to have lunch with the guy.

Instead of subsidizing your cheap friends and coworkers, how about trying something new? What if when sitting down for lunch, everyone at the table agrees to pay his or her fair share? If someone doesn't, each person at the table not only has the right but is expected to say something. *"Okay all you tightwads. We're short $8.00. Pony up for tax and tip. We had a deal."* And if you want to be a bit more tactful, you could say, *"We're short $8.00. If you didn't add tax and tip, please throw in a couple more dollars."*

If you make an agreement in advance, you might feel freer speaking up than if you hadn't made that agreement in the first place.

Why do people continue to stiff you on the bill? Why are they always late? Because you allow it.

When there's no permission to speak candidly, you don't. Most of us are afraid of damaging our relationships. So instead of saying what we really think, we suck it up and wait for people who are late and subsidize people who think that tax and tip don't apply to them.

BEHAVIOR **GUIDELINES**

A few months ago I was speaking at a conference, and two women sitting in the third row talked throughout my entire presentation. The noise drove me nuts. But did I speak to them or confront them? Did I ask them to stop talking? No!

I wanted to say something but I didn't feel that I could— because I hadn't initially requested that the audience refrain from side-talking. If I had asked the two women to stop talking, I would have been criticizing them for something I hadn't asked them not to do. Kind of like getting feedback during a performance appraisal about an issue that no one mentioned to you during the entire year. We all hate that, don't we?

How about asking someone who is texting during a meeting to turn off her phone? When no behavior guidelines are established at the onset of the meeting, how does the facilitator manage participants' behavior?

People feel betrayed when they are called out in these situations, because they're being held to standards they weren't aware of, which makes it impossible for them to win.

You might be thinking these are such common guidelines that they shouldn't even need to be mentioned. Everyone knows we should turn off our phones and not side-talk during presentations. That's true, and yet we break the rules all the time. How many meetings do you attend in which people are stealthily texting under the table, as if no can see what they're doing?

Setting expectations at the beginning of anything new—a meeting, a relationship, or a project—makes it easier to address frustrating behaviors when they happen. And they will happen.

PREPARE FOR THINGS TO GO WRONG

As human beings, we make commitments and then we forget them. How many times have you remembered a meeting only when a reminder popped up in an email? It's why we chose to carry five-pound Franklin planners before replacing them with iPhones and Droids. Our tendency to break commitments is also why personal trainers make a living.

Of course, we don't need someone to watch us warm up on a treadmill and do repetitions. Personal trainers stay in business because without someone expecting us to show up at the gym and charging us if we don't, many of us would sit on our couch watching reruns of bad TV shows.

Rather than expecting people to remember and keep all of their commitments, you're a wise person when you expect that they won't and put what I call a *prevention* in place.

PREVENTIONS

Preventions take into account that people are human and that human beings make mistakes. Let's say you've made a commitment not to eat sugar. You know that if you buy a pint of your favorite ice cream and put it in your freezer, it will be gone in a few days. So, as a prevention, you don't bring ice cream or other desserts into your house. If you're desperate for a sugar fix you may find yourself driving to the nearest convenience store, but leaving your house is definitely less convenient than walking to your freezer.

Since the day after those two women side-talked throughout my presentation, I've taken a few moments to set expectations at the beginning of every speech, training program, and meeting. I ask people to please silence their phones and not side-talk, email, or text during the presentation. Then I put a prevention in place.

I write the agreements down and post them someplace visible at the beginning of every meeting and presentation. I revisit the agreements before breaks and at the onset of each ensuing session. Keeping agreed-upon behaviors in the forefront makes managing "bad" behavior easier. Instead of being the bad guy and reprimanding people, I am merely reminding them of what they've already agreed to do.

Although I establish my presentation and meeting guidelines and then post them, I know some attendees will still talk to the person next to them and whip out their iPhones. They can't help themselves. So I put a *fallback* in place.

FALLBACKS

A fallback is a consequence that a group agrees to when people violate agreements. A typical fallback for meetings is for each person who is late to put a dollar in a jar. When the jar is full, the people who were late have funded a happy hour!

When I managed training sessions for a mutual fund company, I would give participants who arrived late to the training sessions the option of putting a dollar into a jar, singing a song, or telling a joke. All of these agreed-upon fallbacks were effective until people started to purposefully arrive late so they could sing! They wanted their moment of stardom. When I realized that the consequence had become a perk, we agreed on a new fallback.

As we all know, relationships are not always smooth. Unless you're hanging out with androids, you will eventually disappoint someone and be disappointed. Setting expectations, putting *preventions* and *fallbacks* in place, and asking for permission to give and receive feedback are examples of deliberately designing your relationships. Regardless of what happens, each person involved in making the agreement has the freedom to talk about violated expectations. Hopefully this will preserve and strengthen your relationships, so you don't wind up fired or so others don't refuse to work with you, with no explanation.

ASK FOR **CANDOR**

When I was trying to brand my business, the owner of a marketing agency I was considering hiring put a sizable proposal in front of me. I was overwhelmed. The plan was, shall we say, much more robust than I had anticipated. In fact, the cost was a showstopper.

After we learned more about each other's businesses and talked through the elements of the proposal, I said, "Let's talk about money. The cost associated with this proposal overwhelmed me. I'd love to do this work with you, but if I choose to do it, I'll have to go live with my mom."

Despite the fact he had just discovered that I probably couldn't afford to work with him, the owner of the agency looked relieved and said, "Most people dance uncomfortably around the issue of money and never quite get to it. You just threw it out there."

I told him what I tell all the vendors I work with: "I'm really direct. You can say anything to me, and I hope you will. I mean it. Never be worried about something you want or need to say."

So how about trying something new? At the beginning of all of your professional relationships, ask people to be honest with you. Give your boss, coworkers, customers, and vendors permission to say whatever they need to say, and ask for permission to do the same.

EFFECTIVE BUSINESS RELATIONSHIP LANGUAGE

Consider using the following language when starting business relationships.

Kicking Off Relationships with Coworkers

"I want a good relationship with you. If we work together long enough, I'm sure I'll screw it up. I'll wait too long to reply to

an email, make a mistake, or miss a deadline. I'd like the kind of relationship in which we can talk about these things. I always want to know what you think. And I promise that no matter what you tell me, I'll say thank you. Is it okay if I work this way with you?"

Kicking Off Relationships with Direct Reports

"As your manager, my job is to help you get where you want to go, whether that is within this organization or elsewhere. As a result, I'm going to let you know anything I hear you say or see you do or see you wear that either contributes to your success or gets in the way of it."

Managers who take the time and make the effort to set expectations build trust, rapport, and relationship—the elements of smooth working relationships.

Kicking Off Relationships with Direct Supervisors

"I'm committed to my professional development, and I'm always looking for growth opportunities. I hope that if you hear me say or see me do or see me wear anything that gets in the way of how I want to be seen, you will tell me. I promise I'll be receptive and say thank you. I also, of course, hope you'll tell me the things I do well that are in line with your expectations."

Although supervisors don't need permission to give their direct reports feedback, many are hesitant to do so. They don't want to offend or damage a new relationship. Like most people, managers are concerned that if they give negative feedback, they won't be liked or their employees might quit.

You might be thinking, *"It's my boss's job to give me feedback. I shouldn't have to ask for it."* And you're right. Your boss should give you feedback and you shouldn't have to ask for it. But if he doesn't, you're at a huge disadvantage. You may spend massive amounts of time on projects that aren't really important. You may not be given opportunities and never know why. And you may think your performance is strong, only to find out otherwise when you receive a mediocre performance review and a nominal pay increase. So yes, your boss should give you feedback without your having to ask for it. You can be right all day, but your righteousness won't get you any closer to the career or business relationship you want.

THE SCHOOL OF WHAT WORKS VERSUS
THE SCHOOL OF WHAT'S RIGHT

When I was twenty-three, I moved to Boulder, Colorado, because the weather is beautiful and it's never humid in Boulder. I landed my first real job there (my parents were very relieved), supporting trainers who taught public seminars all over the country.

The company sent me to Chicago for training on my first day on the job. I was traveling with my new boss, who was only about six months older than I was and, in my opinion, very snooty. One afternoon we were sitting at a red light at a four-way intersection, waiting to turn right. I had just started to turn when a car in the opposing lane made a left turn and cut me off. I instantly hit the brakes.

My boss scowled and said, "Why did you stop? You had the right of way." I replied, "I'd rather be alive than right."

That experience stuck with me much longer than the job. Since that day, I've worked hard to live by the teachings of *the school of what works* as opposed to *the school of what's right*. That means that rather than stand on a principle, I make sure to get what I need.

Yes, your boss should tell you what he wants at the beginning of your relationship and give you feedback when you violate his expectations. But some managers will do that and some won't. If you want to get more detailed feedback than the statement "*meets expectations*" on your performance appraisal, you must know what your boss wants and how he wants it, as well as his perceptions of your performance.

When you tell your boss you want his feedback and promise to take it graciously, you're saying several things. First, you respect him and his opinion. Second, you demonstrate that you care about your career and take your job seriously. Third, you make it easy to give you feedback. Your boss doesn't have to worry that you're going to get defensive.

So be smart and take your performance into your own hands. Regardless of who you work for or what you think of him or her, ask for feedback early in the relationship. Promise to accept his or her response graciously.

Starting relationships by giving permission to give you feedback may feel a little weird. If my sample conversations feel awkward or unrealistic, use whatever language you feel comfortable with. Choose whatever words seem best to you. The important thing is to get out in front of your relationships.

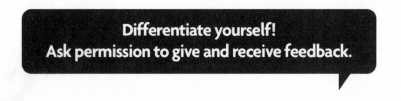

**Differentiate yourself!
Ask permission to give and receive feedback.**

Think about it—has anyone ever overtly given you permission to say whatever you need to say? Or promised that when you do, they'll say thank you? Setting the expectation that you'll give and receive feedback at the beginning of a relationship is so unusual, it immediately sets you apart. Almost no one does this, but everyone wants to work with people who do. Be that person. It's easy and costs absolutely nothing.

As Stephen Covey said in *The 7 Habits of Highly Effective People*, "You're depositing into the emotional bank account." Although trust can be broken in an instant, it is built over time. Since all long-lasting relationships are built on trust, you're laying the foundation for relationships that survive inevitable miscommunications, violated expectations, and other missteps.

Remember: No matter how hard you try, you *will* make mistakes. If a relationship lasts long enough, at some point you'll take too long to return a call, provide misinformation, or disappoint the other person in another way. Wouldn't you like your boss to tell you when you make a mistake, giving you a chance to make things right before getting that bad review or perhaps being fired?

SUMMARY: *GIVE PEOPLE PERMISSION TO TELL YOU THE TRUTH.*

Despite the abundance of training programs on giving and receiving feedback, speaking up in organizations remains difficult, and many people don't do it. We tend to think it's too difficult to confront people. We don't want to deal with the conflict, so we say nothing.

Be smarter. Rather than waiting for something to go wrong, set clear expectations at the beginning of working relationships and projects. Tell your coworkers you want to have a good relationship with them. Make an agreement that when challenges arise, it's not only okay but also expected to discuss what's going on. Agreeing to talk about difficult situations before they happen makes it more likely that when breakdowns occur, you'll be able to speak up with less anxiety.

CHAPTER 2

YOU GET WHAT YOU ASK FOR

One of my biggest training and consulting clients is an accounting firm. In addition to processing tax returns, they audit businesses. Audits require detail-oriented and tedious work plus a big commitment by the company being audited. Being audited is one of those necessary evils, like going to the dentist and getting a filling. It's not fun, but it is necessary.

Accounting firms are all too familiar with the things that will derail an audit—clients who aren't prepared, too few employees assigned to the audit, staffing changes, and more. These things are predictable. They happen regularly.

DEFINE HOW YOU WILL WORK WITH OTHERS
BEFORE PROBLEMS OCCUR

One day I heard a few of my client's employees complaining about a company they were auditing. "This client is never prepared. Every year it's the same thing. We allocate people to the audit, show up on-site, and the client isn't ready. There is no work for us to do. We come back to our office and have a team of people with nothing to do. And the client wonders why we go over budget and the audit isn't finished on schedule."

I asked whether they had ever talked to the client about this lack of preparedness.

One of the auditors explained, "All clients get an engagement letter detailing our audit practices before the audit begins."

My reply: "Yes, I know. But who has an actual conversation with the client before the audit begins? That's when all the pitfalls that can derail the audit should be discussed and when what needs to take place during the audit should be communicated to ensure the audit stays on track and on budget."

The auditor replied, "It's not our place to have that conversation with the client. The partner who sold the engagement needs to do it. It's a status thing. We're low on the totem pole. The client isn't going to listen to us."

The client's CFO received the written letter of agreement. But the CFO wasn't working with the audit team on a daily basis; his staff was working on the audit. And I would bet a lot of money that the CFO's employees never saw the letter of agreement.

What's missing in this situation is a *verbal contract*, agreed upon at the onset of the engagement, that outlines how the client and the audit team will work together. That conversation needs to happen with every person working on the audit. It's not a conversation for just the audit partner and the CFO to have.

In the case of my client, neither the audit team nor their client had set expectations of who was responsible for what or how issues that arose during the audit would be addressed. Could the auditors working on-site with the client discuss issues that arose? Or could only partners have those conversations? Was the client clear about the consequences of not following audit procedures? Was the client told explicitly that if they weren't prepared when the audit team arrived, the audit would cost more?

Clients receive a written contract and a letter of agreement. But a letter doesn't have the impact of a conversation. How many times have you argued with your bank, credit card company, or cell phone provider only to find out later that the terms of your agreement were clearly spelled out in the fine print?

Most business relationships lack a verbal contract outlining who does what and how issues that arise will be managed. So when problems occur, people feel they can't speak up.

It is an all too common scenario.

THE CONSEQUENCES OF
INSUFFICIENT EXPECTATIONS

Here is an example of how internal business relationships go awry when expectations are insufficiently laid out.

Lisa, an internal HR recruiter, is conducting a search for Carol, a hiring manager. Lisa doesn't get enough information from Carol when the job is posted. As a result, Lisa sources candidates who aren't appropriate for the position. Carol rejects every candidate she meets and finally decides that Lisa is incompetent. Lisa decides that Carol is difficult to work with and asks to support a different department. The two never speak to each other about their frustrations.

Does this scenario sound crazy? Of course! Yet it happens all the time.

If, at the onset of the search, Lisa and Carol had asked more questions about what was important to each person, had agreed to periodically talk about how the search was progressing, and had given feedback when things weren't going well, their mutual dissatisfaction and the unfortunate outcome might have been avoided.

Here's another example.

Let's say you're a member of a five-person team working on a project with a tight deadline. You're all pulling together, working hard—except for Jeff, who comes in late, surfs the Internet half the day, and walks around the office chatting with people during the other half. The team is frustrated and talks about Jeff behind his back. No one speaks to Jeff directly, because that's too awkward. And no one wants to be the one who outs the guy to the team leader.

If, during the project kick-off meeting, the team had discussed and come to an agreement about how they would handle frustrations, and specifically what they would do when team members didn't pull their weight, someone might have stepped up and spoken directly to Jeff. But because the team didn't establish these expectations, they all found it easier and more comfortable to do the guy's work than tell him what a slacker he was.

If all of these people—the audit team, the recruiter, the hiring manager, and the project team—had set expectations when they began working together, people would have been clearer about their roles and might have felt freer to speak up when challenges occurred.

SETTING **EXPECTATIONS**

Follow the steps below to successfully set expectations with clients, coworkers, or your boss during a one-on-one conversation or at a project kick-off meeting.

STEP ONE: State your goal.
> *"We want a great relationship. We want our work together to be easy and smooth."*

STEP TWO: Set expectations.
> *"Let's have a conversation and agree on roles and responsibilities so everyone is clear about who will do what."*

STEP THREE: Agree on how you will work together.
> *"Let's talk about how we will address challenges. Things will happen that we don't anticipate. We'd like to be able to talk about any challenge that arises—as it occurs—and not have anyone take anything personally."*

STEP FOUR: Ask for feedback.
> *"Anyone can say anything at any time. We all want the project to go well, and we need to know on a regular basis how you feel things are going. Knowing what's working and not working will allow us to*

make improvements. We should all periodically check in and ask for feedback."

STEP FIVE: Ask for permission to give feedback.

"If we have concerns at any point during the project, we'd like to be able to speak up and have you trust that we are speaking from our commitment to your business and the project and from our desire for this process to go smoothly."

STEP SIX: Agree on roles.

"Let's also discuss who will be having those conversations. Should particular leaders have the discussions, or is it okay for anyone on the project to give feedback at any time? Either way is fine. We just want to be clear so people know what to do and what to expect."

STEP SEVEN: Agree on the communication process.

"Let's agree on in what way, specifically, and how frequently we'll check in to assess progress and evaluate how our working relationship is going."

Watch videos of how to set expectations at:
www.leadershipandsalestraining.com/sayanything

EXAMPLES OF **SETTING EXPECTATIONS WITH EXISTING CLIENTS**

"We've been working together for a while. We want to have a good relationship with you. We want you to be able to say anything to us and vice versa. If you have concerns, we want to know. If you have questions, please ask them. We will always be receptive. And we'd like to be able to do the same with you.

"Regardless of how well we plan, unforeseen things are going to happen. You'll get busy. Staff changes may occur. Deadlines may be

missed. If things get off track or we have concerns, we'd like your permission to say something. Are you comfortable with that? Who would you prefer we talk with?

"We will periodically check in and ask how the work and our working relationship are going. Again, please be candid. We want your feedback, and we want this process to proceed as smoothly and as easily as possible for you."

EXAMPLES OF **SETTING EXPECTATIONS AMONG TEAM MEMBERS**

STEP ONE: Tell your peers.

"I want a good working relationship with you."

STEP TWO: Ask for an open relationship and for feedback when you violate or when you exceed team members' expectations.

When I have this kind of conversation with a peer, I use more casual language. I say something like, *"I'd like a candid relationship where we can say anything and not be worried. If you see me do anything that's going to get in my way, please tell me. If I do anything that annoys you, please tell me. I promise to take it well and not freak out. Is that all right with you?"*

An even more casual approach might be, *"I want things to go well for me here. If you see me do anything stupid, I want you to tell me. Does that work for you? And I'll do the same for you, if you want me to."*

I bet you are thinking, *"There's no way I'd ever say that to one of my coworkers. She or he would think I was weird."* But in my experience, people don't question it. They say, *"Okay, sure,"* and think, *"Well duh, of course we'll both say something if we see each other do something stupid."* Yet we've all seen our coworkers make career-limiting moves at work—showing up unprepared at meetings, wearing clothes that are too casual for work, or leaving early when the rest of the team is still in the office. But saying something about it just felt too awkward, so we didn't.

It's not the language you use that's important. It's that you have the conversation. Candid relationships don't just happen. We sometimes think, *"I don't know her well enough to tell her that she's getting a reputation as someone who never follows through. When we know each other better, I'll be honest. But until then, I'll keep my opinions to myself."*

Once you have a relationship with someone, you've got something to lose. If you're honest and the other person gets upset, you risk harming the relationship. Laying the groundwork for candor at the beginning of the relationship reduces the likelihood of such harm and makes it easier to have difficult conversations later.

STEP THREE: Agree on roles and responsibilities and how often you'll check in to evaluate how the working relationship and the project are going.

For example, *"I want to be clear on what I and the rest of the team are doing. Can we walk through each person's responsibilities, make sure we're all clear and in agreement, and decide how and with what frequency we'll check in and assess progress?"*

Yes, I really do this at the beginning of most of my relationships. When I don't and unexpected things happen, even I am sometimes daunted by challenges as I try to speak up.

I heard through the grapevine that Chloe, a friend who runs a small IT consulting firm, had recently been fired by one of her biggest clients. When Chloe landed the account, she did a great job. After the initial work was done, she turned the account over to one of her direct reports, who, according to the client, did not do a good job. The client fired Chloe's company as a vendor.

I had known Chloe for about a year when I heard about the firing. We made no agreement at the beginning of our friendship that if we had feedback for each other we would say so, regardless of how difficult it might be. As a result, when I heard she'd been fired, and why, I didn't feel like I could say anything.

Instead, over lunch one day, I casually said, "Hey, I heard you were working with Micro Graphics. How is that going?"

Chloe explained, "Oh, they decided to get the work done internally. We're not working with them anymore."

Chloe's client hadn't been candid about why her company was fired. She was unaware of the real reason she had lost the account. And I didn't tell her what I knew. I didn't feel I could. For me to feel comfortable telling Chloe what really happened, we would have had to agree to be candid about things we heard about each other.

The good news is we can still set those expectations. It's never too late.

I can, at any time, say to Chloe, *"At the beginning of most of my relationships I typically ask permission to give and receive feedback, and I make an agreement that if anything happens we think the other person should know, we will both say something. I'm sorry I didn't suggest this when we first met. Do you want to make that agreement now? If anything happens we think the other person should know, we'll each say something, even if it's hard. What do you think?"*

Doing this allows me to tell Chloe why her client fired her, which gives her the opportunity to improve her business. If I really care about the friendship, I'll set this expectation now. If I don't, I probably won't.

SUMMARY: *PLAN FOR BREAKDOWNS BEFORE THEY HAPPEN.*

Set expectations with your internal and external clients at the onset of your working relationships. Rather than expecting everything in your office to go well, assume that breakdowns will happen and plan for them.

Agree on how you'll handle challenges when they arise. Talk about how to avoid difficulties and how to make it more likely that your work together will go smoothly. Ask permission to give feedback. Asking for what you want up front makes missteps and upsets less likely and makes it easier to talk about challenges when they happen.

CHAPTER 3

TAKING THE MYSTERY OUT OF **WORKING WITH OTHERS**

At age twenty-five, I was offered a position selling training for a national leadership development training and consulting firm. The catch? I had never sold anything in my life and knew absolutely nothing about sales. The job offer was contingent on my willingness to live in Fort Collins, a town in northern Colorado, just south of the Wyoming border. I was scared to take a job doing something at which I had no experience, in a town I'd never seen. But I was eagerly trying to break into the world of training and development and really wanted the opportunity. Although terrified, I accepted the job and moved to Fort Collins.

So far, so good, right?

About four weeks into the job, I received a call from my boss in the Denver office, which is about eighty miles south of Fort Collins. Furious, he yelled, "Where are you? It's been four weeks and I haven't seen you."

I told him I was in Fort Collins, getting acclimated and calling on potential clients. I was doing my job, or so I thought.

Still yelling, he replied, "Fort Collins? You're living in Fort Collins? All new employees are on probation for the first ninety days of employment. You haven't earned the right to move to Fort Collins. I was going to tell you when you had permission to move."

That was news to me.

He continued, "I want to see you in my office every Friday at two o'clock. I want to know who you've called, who you've seen, and exactly what you're doing. It's very clear I can't trust you." And then he hung up the phone.

Ouch!

Although upsetting, that experience taught me something that, fifteen years later, is still one of the most valuable career lessons I've ever learned.

My boss never told me to wait ninety days to move. He never told me he wanted to see me each week. He never told me I should track and report all of my calls and appointments.

He just expected me to know.

Unfortunately, that situation was not unique. Each time I joined a new company, I found out all over again how long it takes to learn how to work with people and what happens when you don't know others' work habits and preferences. Finally, I got tired of learning the hard way and took my business relationships, career satisfaction, and success into my own hands—where it belongs.

DON'T **GUESS**

I started a list of everything I could remember *assuming* and not clarifying about the people I worked with. As time went by, whenever I made another assumption, I added it to the list. What started as a handwritten list on one of those little hotel notepads is now a twelve-page, single-spaced, typewritten list.

In the next few chapters, I'll share many of the questions I've developed to eliminate unfounded assumptions. I'm hoping to help you avoid the guessing, frustration, and damaged relationships often inherent in working with new people.

Figuring out how to work with people takes time. Depending on how open or communicative new bosses or new customers are, it can take years of trial and error to learn how best to work with them. Do they prefer communicating via email or via voicemail? Would they rather schedule appointments or have impromptu conversations? Do they work better in the morning or in the afternoon, or even at night?

When we don't know how people like to work, we guess and then usually treat them the way we like to be treated. If you like the phone, you'll call. If you prefer to structure your time, you'll work by appointment. But it's not about you. It's about your boss, your coworkers, and your customers. When the people you work with get what they need, you will get what you need. The problem is that most people won't tell you when you fail to accommodate their preferences. Rather than make requests or give you feedback, the people you work with are likely to be frustrated in silence. But they may complain about you behind your back, work around you, or even fire you.

AVOID MISSTEPS BY ASKING ABOUT WORK HABITS AND PREFERENCES

When beginning to work with a new set of people, avoid unforeseen missteps and shorten the inherent learning curve by asking about their work habits and preferences.

Several years ago I hired a manager who reported to me. She was in Texas; I was in Colorado. Five weeks into her employment, she gave me some very clear feedback.

She called and said, "When you hired me, you said you cared about your employees, and you genuinely seemed to care. But now I'm not so sure. I sent you an email ten days ago and have not received a reply. I sent it again last week; still no reply."

I wanted my new employee to feel good about working for the company and with me, but in a matter of weeks, my behavior had her questioning her decision to join the team. At that time, I received at least 150 emails a day. Do the math: If I took three minutes to open, read, and reply to every email, I would spend 7.5 hours reading email every day. So I gave up trying to respond quickly and replied to emails whenever I could.

My mistake was not that I didn't keep up with my email (although my boss might have disagreed). My error was in not setting the appropriate expectation with my staff. All I needed to do was to tell my employees, *"I get a lot of email and am usually slow to respond. If you don't hear back from me in a timely way, it's not personal and doesn't mean you and your messages aren't important. If you need to reach me, please call me. I respond to voicemails much more quickly than email."*

That message was clear and easy to share, but I hadn't imparted it. It didn't occur to me, until I had damaged a relationship I needed to nurture.

At my next organization, I had an employee who emailed me about absolutely everything he was doing and copied me on messages I didn't need to see. I was overwhelmed by all the communication and couldn't discern what was important. Fortunately, I had learned from my previous mistake.

I called him and said, "Mike, I appreciate you keeping me in the loop, but I'm a little overwhelmed by all the communications you've sent me. As a result, I'm not getting to the things that are most important. I want to be sure I'm reading and replying to the things you need my input on. Rather than share all of your projects, just send me the items that are most important and tell me when you would like my input. That way, you'll get the attention you deserve."

Yes, I felt awkward telling Mike to be more judicious with his communications; I wanted to be accessible and available to him. But what's worse—telling Mike I can't read all of his emails, or ignoring every message and having him wonder whether he's communicating into a black hole?

IT'S NO BIG DEAL TO YOU

Walk around your office and you'll hear people complaining about things that may seem trivial to you but are a big deal to them—conference rooms left a mess, borrowed office supplies, or chairs taken elsewhere for a meeting and never returned.

We can laugh, but these types of office faux pas can create a lasting impression. It would be unfortunate if a colleague decides you're inconsiderate because you borrowed his chair and didn't return it. And as a result of this minor misstep, when he assembles a team for the next project, you're not on it.

I'm not suggesting you tiptoe around your office, afraid to upset your coworkers. Just the opposite. Don't guess or assume what others find frustrating—ask them. Teach people how to work with you by telling them how you like to work and by asking how they prefer to work with you.

After I tell people I want a good and candid relationship in which both of us can speak freely, I ask permission to ask a few questions. Then I get specific as I inquire about their working-style preferences.

ASKING YOUR COWORKERS ABOUT THEIR
WORKING-STYLE PREFERENCES

Below are questions that you can ask coworkers, fellow team members, and direct supervisors to get a clear sense of their working styles.

1. How do you best like to communicate? Via email, voicemail, text message, instant messenger, telephone, or in person?

2. Are you a morning, afternoon, or night person?

3. If we need to talk, do you prefer to work by appointment or would you prefer I drop by your office or give you a call?

4. If I need to reach you outside of regular business hours, what method is best? What time is too early and what time is too late to call?

5. How do you feel about being called on your cell phone?

6. What are your pet peeves? What types of things annoy you at work?

7. How will I know when you're frustrated?

8. If I need something quickly, how do you prefer to be interrupted?

9. If I have something to give you when you're not in your office, where would you prefer I leave it? On your desk or chair, or in your in-box or with your assistant?

These questions address the simple things that can make working with other people easy or frustrating. When violated, these preferences tend to cause big problems.

There is one hard-and-fast rule here: You cannot introduce these questions via email.

Taking the time to ask about another person's working-style preferences is a rapport builder. Emailing a list of questions is not. Asking these questions is as much about having the dialogue as it is about getting the information. If you email a list of questions about working-style preferences, people may make the wrong assumptions. They may think, *"The company is laying off workers, and they're using these questions to determine who will be the first to go."*

Build rapport; don't break it. Ask these questions either in person or, for remote relationships, over the phone. The purpose is to address basic working-style preferences. Use the questions you like and omit the ones you don't. If you like a question but don't like how it is worded, rewrite it. The point isn't what you ask. The point is that you *do* ask.

> **Watch videos of how to introduce the working-style preference questions at:**
> www.leadershipandsalestraining.com/sayanything

EXAMPLES OF **BUILDING RAPPORT**

My last boss was a morning person. I'm a night person. He was in the office by 7:00 a.m. each day and left by 6:00 p.m. When he left work, he really left. He didn't check his email or his voicemail after hours, and his wife had a "no BlackBerry in the house" rule.

I never walked into the office before 9:00 a.m. (okay, 9:30) and would have been happy if conference calls were held at 10:00 p.m. My boss probably went to sleep just when I was getting my second wind.

I knew I would eventually need to talk to my boss at night but had no idea how to reach him. Was it okay to call his home number? Under what circumstances? Until what time could I call? I could have stewed over those questions for months, waiting until I had an emergency and then not knowing what to do.

Instead, I simply asked him, "If I need to reach you at night, is it okay to call? Until what time and what number should I call? Should I call only in the event of an emergency, or is it okay to call with simple questions?" I was rewarded with my boss's home number and the clear instruction to call only if it was really important and not past 10:00 p.m.

This turned out to be the hardest job I'd ever had. One night a year into it, I was having a "moment." One of my colleagues had done something so frustrating that, had I been able to do so, I would have fired the guy. Instead, I looked at my watch—it was 9:30 p.m. I called my boss's home number.

I'll never forget that conversation. I was standing on a curb outside a grocery store, yelling, "This job is like swimming upstream alone, wearing ski clothes!"

My boss talked me down off the ledge and into a solution. And I felt better, much better than if I hadn't asked and received permission to call after hours in an emergency situation.

Don't be caught during a "moment" not knowing if or how you can reach your boss. Don't spend months or years trying to figure out how people like to communicate. Just ask. Make your working relationships smoother and demonstrate that you care about what's important to your colleagues and employees.

Here are a few more questions to help you get to know the people you work with better:

1. When is your birthday?

2. What is your favorite hobby, type of food, and store in which to shop?

3. What are you concerned about at work?

4. What questions do you have for me?

When I teach this concept in organizations, I almost always get the objection that the first two questions are nice but not useful. I wish I was that nice, but I don't do things at work that don't have a purpose. The first two questions allow you to acknowledge people in a way that they usually like. Most people appreciate having their birthday recognized. You don't have to do anything big—a birthday email or voicemail does the job.

Eventually someone you work with will go out of her way for you or will accomplish something big. Buying a gift certificate to her favorite store or restaurant sends a very loud message—you cared enough to learn and remember her preferences. Buying a Starbucks gift card for someone who doesn't drink coffee sends an equally strong message—you don't know her preferences and never cared enough to find out.

Of course, you can't remember everyone's birthday or favorite restaurant. Start a paper or electronic file for each person you work with and put answers to the questions in the file. When you need to "remember" something, consult the file. Personally, I love the messages I get thanking me for remembering people's birthdays. But I don't truly "remember" birthdays. (I can barely remember my own birthday.) I just put an annual reminder in Outlook and it remembers for me. If the date doesn't make it into Outlook, there's always Facebook.

The last two questions are catchall questions. You've opened the door to candid communication; as a result, people will likely feel free to discuss other issues with you. Asking for their concerns and other things they want to know gives people an opportunity to expand the conversation with you into areas that are important to them.

You don't need to ask all the questions. You want to get to know people, not interrogate them. Some people enjoy conversations like this and will welcome all of the questions. Others won't have the patience or see the point. If the person you are talking to seems interested and offers more information, feel free to ask more questions. If the person appears rushed, ask a few questions and move on to another topic. You can ask additional questions at a future meeting. You don't need to know everything immediately.

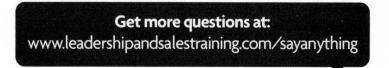

Get more questions at:
www.leadershipandsalestraining.com/sayanything

It's ideal to ask these questions when a relationship begins, but it's never too late and it doesn't have to be awkward. Just as you can always ask permission to give and receive feedback, you can always ask about another person's working-style preferences. You can do it formally, during a meeting, or informally, sprinkling questions into conversations.

Consider saying something like this to longtime coworkers:

"We've been working together for a long time, and yet there are things about you I don't know that I'd like to know, like some of your working-style preferences and the things that tend to frustrate you. Would it be okay if I ask you a few questions?"

"I typically email you when I need something. Does that work for you, or would you prefer me to call or swing by your office?"

"I always create our meeting agendas. I realized we've never talked about how you'd like to manage our department's meetings. Should I continue writing the agendas or would you like to do something different?"

People love talking about themselves. When you ask about their working-style preferences, you demonstrate an interest and a desire to accommodate their needs. Who wouldn't welcome that?

A TRUE-LIFE **SCENARIO**

Several years ago I flew from Denver to New York with a new boss. As we were planning the trip, I mentioned the list of questions I'd written to create smoother working relationships. I asked if she would be willing to talk through them during the flight. She agreed. On the day of our flight, I handed her the list of questions, and we had an amazing conversation, opening the door to a fantastic relationship.

My next boss was quite the opposite. Had I asked for a meeting to discuss working-style preferences and walked into his office with a list of questions, he would have laughed "me and my touchy-feely, training garbage" right into the hallway. Not to be deterred, whenever I met with him, I slipped a question or two into our conversation. It was a little like disguising a vegetable with melted cheese so a kid would eat it. Eventually, I learned what I needed to know.

Here are some additional ways to introduce a conversation about working-style preferences:

"I want a good relationship with you and would like us to get to know each other better. Is it okay if I ask you a few questions about your working-style preferences? We can talk now or schedule time on another day."

Or, *"Because we're going to work together pretty frequently, I thought it would be good to talk about our working-style preferences. Would that be okay with you? We can talk now or schedule time on another day."*

Or, *"I'd like to be easy to work with. Would it be okay to ask each other a few questions about our working-style preferences so we know how to work together and don't inadvertently drive each other crazy?"*

Again, always use language that fits you and your personality. How you introduce the questions isn't important. It's just important that you ask. The questions can be asked during one-on-one conversations, in teams, or in groups. One of my favorite things to do during team meetings is to pick a question and have each person on the team answer it. At the next meeting, I pick a different question and everyone answers that question.

> Going bowling won't help teams work better together.
> **Asking about working-style preferences will.**

Answering questions as a team helps team members learn about each other quickly, and it creates camaraderie. But some of us think we can't ask about others' working-style preferences, let alone expect people to accommodate *our* preferences. Why not?

If you're going to have candid and real relationships at work, you need to be able to make requests. People won't necessarily honor your requests, but they definitely won't if they don't know what your requests are.

SUFFERING IS **OPTIONAL**

Giving people permission to talk about the things that drive them crazy and to make requests is one step toward creating an open atmosphere in which people can speak freely.

One thing that drives me absolutely nuts is pen clicking—pushing the button on the top of a pen up and down or clicking the cap on and off or tapping a pen on a table. Does this make me sound high maintenance? Please allow me to explain.

I'm an auditory learner, so I find noise like this really distracting. Instead of focusing on the discussion in a meeting, I'm preoccupied with strategizing how I can get the hyperactive guy to put down his damn pen.

If the people I work with held a conversation about pet peeves and gave each other permission to make a request when someone does something that makes them crazy, it would be easier for me to lean over and ask the pen tapper to give it a rest. Without this context, if I say something to the pen tapper, the guy will probably think I'm a jerk.

> **Pave the way to candid relationships by granting people permission to tell you the truth.**

Feeling comfortable speaking up and making requests is all about granting permission. When we've openly talked about our preferences and given our colleagues permission to make requests, doing so becomes easier. Not easy, but easier.

Sharing preferences as a group also ensures that everyone hears the same thing at the same time. Many organizations, managers, and teams have gotten into trouble by using the "whisper-down-the-lane" announcement method—you know, those instances when information is not shared with an entire organization, department, or team simultaneously. Rather, announcements that affect an entire group are shared via different methods and at different times.

This method of sharing information is fraught with pitfalls. The conversations heard in hallways, cubicles, and break rooms sound something like, *"Why did she tell you that? She didn't tell me or the rest of the team that! Why would she have talked only to you?"* Or, *"That's not what I heard. What did you hear?"*

When a company communicates important information in an indirect fashion, perfectly sane people often become paranoid and nervous the moment they walk into their workplace lobby. But well-run organizations allay people's anxiety by being open in how they share information. You and your company are working to build trust. The more open and transparent the communication, the greater the trust will be. The greater the trust, the more open and candid people will be.

What happens if your manager or project manager would never in a million years suggest talking about working-style preferences? Can you have an impact, even if you don't lead the department, team, or meeting?

It's in your best interest to communicate with people at all levels about how they like to communicate. It's good career and reputation management, and it makes your life easier. To email a department head three or four times to get a singular piece of information is time consuming and frustrating. Is she ignoring you? Or does she simply prefer the phone? It's quicker and easier to ask her or her assistant how she likes to communicate.

Are you hesitant to talk to senior people about their preferences, wondering whether you have the right to ask those questions and whether they'll be receptive? Let me allay your concern. Yes, you have the right. And yes, they'll be receptive. Who wouldn't appreciate being asked how he likes to communicate? Anything that makes someone else's life easier is a welcome discussion topic.

WHO ACCOMMODATES WHOM?

Are managers expected to use their direct reports' preferred communication style, or does the manager's title and status entitle the manager to expect employees to accommodate her? If you're an outside salesperson, do your customers accommodate you or do you accommodate your customers?

The answer is simple, if not entirely to your liking. Managers and customers always get preferential treatment. It's just one of those things. They've earned the right. Stay in the business long enough, get promoted to VP, and you too will have people accommodating you. Until then, play along.

If you're a project manager trying to get a meeting with the head of IT, don't tell the guy's assistant you prefer Tuesday mornings. Take whatever he is willing to give you. If your biggest customer wants to meet in person, you get on that plane and go, even if you think the meeting could easily be held over the phone.

Think about the people you want to work with versus the ones you don't.

Most companies have left employees and customers alike behind because they are simply too difficult to work with. When I started my business, one of my first customers was a large company with lots of protocol, policies, and paperwork. I was a contractor, and the person who was overseeing my work was a massive control freak. He questioned and provided input on everything I did. As a result, the work was stressful and not fun. Because of the company's confusing accounts payable policies, it took me twelve hours of phone calls and emails to figure out how to get paid, and five months to receive a check. When our contract was up, I chose not to renew it. It just wasn't worth it.

Regardless of your level or role in an organization, you can always choose to be someone people want to work with.

What does all this discussion about working-style preferences and who asks and accommodates whom have to do with candor?

You've told the people you work with that you want a good relationship. Asking about and accommodating their working-style preferences demonstrates that you mean it. Asking these questions builds trust. People are more candid with those they trust.

SUMMARY: *ASK ABOUT OTHERS' WORKING-STYLE PREFERENCES; DON'T ASSUME.*

When we know how people like to work, we're less likely to violate their expectations and damage relationships. The more you know about people at the beginning of a working relationship, the fewer difficult conversations you will need to have. Consider asking about working-style preferences as a form of conflict prevention.

Creating relationships in which you can say whatever is on your mind without feeling nauseous doesn't happen overnight. It's an iterative process. You tell others you want a good relationship with them, ask permission to give and receive feedback, and then overtly ask about working-style preferences. You're paving the way to powerful working relationships, one step at a time.

CHAPTER 4

HOW TO CREATE **CANDID** MANAGERIAL RELATIONSHIPS

S hould you read this chapter if you're not a manager? YES! Don't you want to know all the dirty, little secrets I'm about to tell your boss?

Did you know that 99.99 percent of employee turnover is predictable? If an employee quits and his manager is surprised, the manager doesn't know his employee as well as he thinks he does. And if an employee isn't succeeding, that too is predictable.

It's possible to have open relationships in which your employees tell you when they're dissatisfied. When employees are candid, they give you the chance to retain them. Without this knowledge, we don't know why seemingly happy employees leave. When you have relationships in which employees tell you the truth about their level of satisfaction, there are no surprises.

SET EXPECTATIONS AND TELL EMPLOYEES WHAT YOU WANT

Another management pitfall is assuming your employees will approach work the same way you do. Perhaps you wouldn't dream of turning work in late and with errors, or taking a vacation day at the busiest time of the year. You assume your employees wouldn't do those things either, but this is not the case.

Our employees are not us, and they don't approach work the way we do. We need to tell employees what we expect and ask what they expect from us, and we need to do this at the beginning of the relationship. Having these conversations early in relationships is much easier than after an employee has disappointed us or is frustrated by some company policy. There is no emotion involved when setting expectations early in a working relationship or project. You're merely stating your expectations and learning theirs.

This chapter is clearly geared toward managers. But if you're not a manager, you'd be wise to keep reading. You may have a manager who sets clear expectations and makes it safe to say whatever you need to say. But it's likely that you don't. There are good managers and there are bad managers. If you work long enough, you'll have both.

You deserve to have a job you enjoy, regardless of whom you work for. The same is true for the managers reading this chapter.

YOU ARE **100 PERCENT** ACCOUNTABLE FOR YOUR CAREER

If you're waiting for your manager to mentor you or help accelerate your career, you may wait a very long time. I want your career to progress and for you to be satisfied, regardless of whom you work for. If your manager doesn't have the conversations with you that are outlined here, you can initiate them. Take charge of your career and your business relationships. Don't wait for someone to make it happen for you.

Direct supervisors and employees both benefit when they take the time to get to know each other better when working relationships begin. What's the best way to do this? By asking simple, direct questions.

QUESTIONS FOR MANAGERS TO ASK NEW DIRECT REPORTS OR TEAM MEMBERS

This is the process I follow when I hire a new employee. First, I say,

> *"As your manager, my job is to help you get where you want to go, whether that's here within this organization or elsewhere. As a result, I'm going to let you know anything I hear you say, see you do, or see you wear that either contributes to where you want to go or gets in the way of that goal."*

You're setting the expectation that you'll be watching your employee's performance and that you'll address positive and negative behavior. And as crazy as it sounds, there are a lot of managers who don't do either of these things. If you've been working for a few years, I'm sure you've had a manager who's told you, "You're doing great. Just keep doing what you're doing." This is nice to hear, but it's not helpful.

In addition to letting employees know they'll receive feedback, you're building trust. We've all gotten feedback that's gone in one ear, out the other, and into the circular file. We listen best to the people we trust who we think have our best interests at heart. Until you build a trusting relationship with your employees, you might as well talk to a wall. The results will be the same.

Then I say,

> *"I want us to have a good relationship and get to know each other better. I'm going to give you a list of questions. Please review it, and in a week we'll have our first one-on-one meeting to discuss the questions. Choose questions on the list that you'd like to ask me, and feel free to add your own questions. I'll answer all the questions I can. If you have questions I can't answer, I'll let you know, and I'll tell you why. Going through this list of questions will help us get to know each other better and will help ensure that our working relationship has a strong start."*

I then hand my employee or project team member the list of questions, and I schedule a follow-up meeting to discuss them.

> Get additional questions and watch videos about how to set expectations with your employees and direct supervisor at:
> **www.leadershipandsalestraining.com/sayanything**

I recommend scheduling one ninety-minute or two forty-five-minute meetings to discuss the questions. That may seem like a lot of time. If it does, consider this—how long does it take to repair a damaged relationship, work the wrong employee out of the organization, or train a new employee? You'll learn a great deal during the conversation—things you could and should have learned during the interview process. The time you invest in starting relationships with clear expectations will save you many hours of frustration.

One of the most frequent requests I get from organizations is for feedback training. The leaders who hire me are concerned that their managers don't give enough feedback and thus employees don't develop or know where they stand performance-wise.

Telling an employee he isn't meeting expectations is not a fun conversation, regardless of how direct you are or how good your relationship with the employee is. Managers who set clear expectations at the beginning of working relationships have fewer difficult conversations. Employees don't have to guess what the manager wants and are thus more likely to deliver results. As William Ury said in his book *Getting to Yes*, "Go slow to go fast." Time spent creating powerful working relationships at the beginning pays off later. I guarantee it.

During my first one-on-one with new employees, I ask a handful of the following Candor Questions®:

1. What are three things that will keep you with the organization?

2. What's the one thing that would make you leave the organization?

3. What three things do you need in a job to be satisfied?

4. What do you enjoy doing most?

5. What is something you want to do that you have never had a chance to do?

6. What skill(s) would you like to develop?

7. How do you like to receive recognition for a job well done—publicly or privately?

8. What would you like to be doing in one year? In three years?

9. Why did you accept this job or role on this project? What are you hoping this job or role will provide?

10. What are your concerns?

11. How will I know when you're frustrated and need support?

12. What do you want to know about me?

13. What else would you like me to know about you?

14. What additional questions do you have?

Each question is basic, simple, and seemingly obvious. You might be thinking, *"Of course, I should ask these questions. How could I not have done so before?"*

I worked in the corporate arena for almost fifteen years, and none of my managers ever asked me these questions. And I had some very good managers. After a few years of struggling to figure out how to work with each manager and learn what each wanted from me, I scheduled meetings and asked the questions myself. I wanted to start the relationships in a positive way rather than violate unstated expectations. Violating a manager's expectations, even expectations she hasn't shared, creates awkwardness and frustration from which it can take months, if not years, to recover.

EMPLOYEES DON'T NEED TO ANSWER ALL THE QUESTIONS

If this is a new relationship, some of these questions may feel a bit risky, and your direct reports may be hesitant to answer them. It may take a few months before employees are comfortable answering all the questions, but that doesn't mean you shouldn't ask them. So few managers ask these questions that you'll get "credit" just for doing so. More important, you're beginning the process of building trust, rapport, and a solid relationship.

If you suspect that your employees will be uncomfortable answering some of the Candor Questions, consider modifying how you ask them. For example, consider saying,

> *"It's okay if you're not comfortable answering all of these questions. I know we're just getting to know each other. You don't need to answer all of them. I just want you to know that I care about and am committed to your success. And I want you to feel comfortable telling me what you need in order to have a good experience here."*

Again, use whatever language you're comfortable with.

THE **TWO MOST IMPORTANT QUESTIONS**

Every manager should be able to answer the following two questions about each of his or her employees. If you can't, I'll go out on a limb and assert that you're not as good a manager as you could be. You're at risk of losing employees and never knowing why.

1. What are three things that will keep you with the organization?

2. What's the one thing that would make you leave the organization?

Your employees are keenly aware of your authority. Even those with whom you have good relationships know you're the boss, and there are some things direct reports just don't say to the boss. Because they fear the consequences, employees often don't state their greatest needs, even when not getting those needs met will drive them out of the organization.

A few years ago, my friend Hilary took a job with a great company, but she eventually came to feel she was in the wrong role. Initially, Hilary had a manager she knew well and was comfortable with. But when her manager moved to a different role within the organization, Hilary began reporting directly to the CEO, whom she didn't know as well and with whom she was not comfortable.

As the months progressed, Hilary became certain she was in the wrong job and became increasingly unhappy. Still not completely comfortable with the CEO, she didn't say anything about her frustration.

Eventually Hilary reached the end of her rope, decided it was time to make a change, and quit. The CEO was shocked and felt betrayed, because Hilary had recently been given an additional department to run. "If you were going to leave, why accept a larger role?" the CEO asked. When Hilary told him that she had been unhappy in her job for a long time and felt misplaced, he was surprised and asked why she hadn't told him. She replied that she was worried about what would happen and how her dissatisfaction would be handled.

While she wasn't open enough with the CEO to give him all of the following details, Hilary thought what all employees think, *"If my boss knows I'm unhappy and there is no other role for me, I'll be dismissed, perhaps not literally but figuratively. I won't be given decent raises or new opportunities if my boss thinks I'm unhappy and thus on my way out. What happens if the company takes action before I'm ready? If I'm going to leave, it's going to be on my own terms."*

Hilary also didn't tell the CEO that he had never asked how she was enjoying her job, what she liked and didn't like about the company, and what it would take to keep her. He assumed that because she was still employed and working hard, everything was fine.

What's the lesson? Most of your mature employees (read: older than thirty) will not tell you what they need or when they're unhappy. Instead, they'll gut it out hoping things will improve. In the meantime, their morale and productivity will drop, because unhappy employees are never as productive as those who are satisfied. And eventually they'll leave. Most young employees won't hang in there for a few years, waiting to see whether things improve. If after a few months they aren't happy and don't see things getting better, they will be out the door and onto the next opportunity.

Get ahead of this predictable but avoidable outcome. Ask your employees what will make them stay and what will make them leave. Revisit these questions regularly, asking about employees' ongoing experiences in their roles and with the organization. This knowledge gives you the power to take action—power most managers don't have, because they don't ask.

NO INFORMATION EQUALS NO POWER

It may feel risky to ask employees what they really want. What if they ask for something you can't provide? For example, what if you discover that having a flexible schedule and the ability to work from home is incredibly important to your new employee, but your company doesn't support telecommuting? While you can't offer her the ability to work from home, knowing this employee's desires allows you to talk about her requests openly and may generate solutions; at the very least, it will keep you from being surprised should she resign.

Perhaps it's not working from home that she really wants—it's the ability to drop her kids off at school or to avoid morning rush hour. If she can commute during off hours, she's content working from the office. If you never have this dialogue and the employee quits, you'll never know why. If it turns out that working from home is really a deal breaker, you'll lose her anyhow. You might as well know at the onset of the relationship, before you waste months and thousands of dollars on training and development.

Asking about employees' desires demonstrates that you take an interest in your employees, want them to be happy, and will do what you can to make that happen. Even if you can't give employees what they want, you get credit and points for asking and having the conversation; it's a conversation that few, if any, managers ever initiate.

HOW, WHEN, AND WHY TO ASK THE QUESTIONS

As managers, we sometimes assume that others want what we want. If we want a flexible work schedule, then others must want one too. If we appreciate recognition in the form of a spot bonus, our employees must want financial rewards as well. If we wouldn't commute for more than forty-five minutes, we can't expect others to do it either. Not the case. People need different things to be happy. If we don't ask them, we'll never know what those things are.

▸ What three things do you need in a job to be satisfied?

A friend who owns a small law firm recently hired his first paralegal. She had ten years of experience and needed no training, which is exactly what Jim wanted. He was busy and needed an employee who could hit the ground running.

When Jim told me he'd hired someone, I asked if he knew what she needed to be happy. He told me about the candy store below their office that sold the most incredible, handmade ice cream. He took his new paralegal there every afternoon. I let Jim know that while his paralegal might like ice cream and appreciate that he bought it for her every day, it might not be what she needed.

I encouraged Jim to ask her why she took the job and what she was hoping it would provide.

Jim indulged me and the next day asked what was important to her. They had an in-depth conversation, unlike any other since she'd started working for him. Jim discovered that his experienced paralegal needed to be constantly learning and growing. If she wasn't adding to her skill set, she would quickly become bored and start hunting for another job. Jim had no idea.

Because she'd been a paralegal for so long, Jim assumed she was content in the role and wasn't looking to learn new things or take on additional responsibilities. Since that conversation, he's been giving her exposure to work outside the typical responsibilities of a paralegal, providing her new insight into the business. While they're still enjoying their afternoon ice cream ritual, Jim now knows what his paralegal needs to be happy and satisfied in her role, in addition to what flavors she likes.

▸ What do you enjoy doing most?

In their book, *Now, Discover Your Strengths*, Marcus Buckingham and Donald Clifton say that employees are likely to stay in jobs where about 75 percent of the time they get to do what they like and feel competent doing. Employees are a turnover risk if they do only what they enjoy or feel competent doing about 25 percent of the time.

For example, if one of your employees loves public speaking, but it's not part of her job, it's only a matter of time before she begins to crave using that skill. If you don't know she enjoys public speaking, you have no reason to provide her an opportunity to do so. But once you are aware of her interest, you can look for opportunities for her to use that skill, even if it's outside the scope of her job—such as presenting on your behalf at meetings and conferences.

Providing opportunities for employees to use their best talents allows you to walk your talk. It demonstrates that you meant what you said during the initial expectation-setting conversation:

> *"As your manager, my job is to help you get where you want to go, whether that's here within this organization or elsewhere . . . and . . . I'm committed to your success and satisfaction."*

▶ **What is something you want to do that you have never had a chance to do?**

▶ **What skill would you like to develop?**

These questions provide a back door to identifying areas in which employees are weak. For example, as embarrassing as this is to admit, I'm lousy at Excel. I can barely do the basics. When I started at a previous job, my boss asked, "You know how to use Excel, right?" Wanting to make the right impression and not wanting to look like an idiot, I said, "Yes, of course," thinking that was the only possible answer. Had he asked what I hadn't had the chance to do or learn, I might have said that I'd like more access to software applications like Excel. Phrasing the question that way is less threatening and wouldn't have made me appear incompetent or ill prepared for my new role.

If you want to learn more about your employees' likes, skills, and areas for potential development, ask questions in such a way that they'll feel safe telling you the answers.

▶ **How do you like to receive recognition for a job well done—publicly or privately?**

An organization I used to work for hosted an "Employee of the Month Lunch." Each month the management team accepted nominations and acknowledged the winner during a ceremony in the company's largest meeting room. There were typically eighty to one hundred attendees, including the winner's team and the organization's eighty leaders and managers. The last month the organization offered the lunch, the winner was so shy she was completely overwhelmed by all the attention. She was so mortified after being brought on stage in front of such a large group that she called in sick for three days following the lunch. The event had the opposite result than what was intended. Rather than feeling rewarded, the employee felt embarrassed and went home.

If the winner's manager had asked the employee how she liked to receive recognition—publicly or privately—the manager would have known that a handwritten note and a gift card would have made the employee feel both comfortable and appreciated.

Don't assume you know how your employees like to receive recognition and don't practice one-size-fits-all recognition programs. Ask employees for their preferences.

▸ **What would you like to be doing in one year? In three years?**

Although it's a horrible interview question, this question is most typically asked when assessing candidates. Obviously, the only right answer is the job the person is interviewing for or the next level job. Unless you're using this question as an intelligence test, I implore you not to ask it during interviews. Instead, ask the question during your initial development and planning conversations to help design a career path that will motivate an employee's long-term commitment to the organization.

▸ **Why did you accept this job?**

▸ **What are you hoping this job will provide?**

If you want to keep your employees for a long time, you need to know where they'd like to take their careers. If a current role won't help an employee get where she wants to go, or if the opportunity to do what she eventually wants to do doesn't exist at the company, it's best to have that discussion when the employee starts working for you. Likewise, if her expectations for the job aren't realistic, it's better to have that conversation right away, rather than after months or years of frustration and disappointment. Again, if you can't give an employee what she needs, it's better to find that out early in her tenure with the company and take one of the following actions:

1. Find the employee another role that will give her what she wants.

2. Agree that this role won't give the employee what she really wants but that it does provide something else, and be sure she is okay with that—really okay with it, rather than just telling you that while she looks for another job.

3. Agree that this role won't give the employee what she wants, but it will help prepare her for a future role and thus is an important career move.

Ideally, you've done such a good job during the hiring process of outlining the job's responsibilities and potential career path that hiring employees who really want to be doing something else is unusual. But it does happen. Helping employees stay with your company and develop for a desired career move, even if it's not within your organization, can be in your best interest, provided the employee stays with you long enough to make a meaningful contribution.

▸ **What are your concerns?**

Candidates will often say whatever they think you want to hear in order to get the job. As a result, quite often candidates don't ask all the questions they have or address all their potential concerns during the interview process. They're eager to make the right impression and don't want to say or do anything that might negatively impact their candidacy. Even internal employees who change jobs within an organization may not know what to ask or be concerned about. Give employees the opportunity to express concerns and ask additional questions once the pressure of interviewing is behind them.

▸ **How will I know when you're frustrated and need support?**

All employees give signals when they're stressed. Some people close the door to their office and ignore incoming calls. Some get sick.

Others work from home to reduce distractions and interruptions. Knowing how to identify when your employees need assistance will help you provide it, without guesswork. Regular meetings and status updates will also ensure that you know where employees stand with projects and initiatives, so you can provide assistance, if necessary.

One of my previous direct reports was as close as I could get to the ideal employee. Stacey was bright and conscientious. She cared as much about our department's outcomes as I did and would do anything I asked—and didn't ask—to ensure we were successful. She was a pleasure to work with in every way. Stacey's only Achilles' heel was that she was a workaholic who didn't communicate when she needed help. When she became overwhelmed with the stress of the job, she got sick and took a week off. And when she got sick, she got really sick. The woman did not mess around.

In hindsight, Stacey and I should have established a method for her to let me know when the stress was getting to her, like saying some code word, or simply coming into my office and telling me that she was overwhelmed and needed help. Encourage your employees not to feel embarrassed or hesitant to come to you when they're stressed or need assistance. It will let them know that you care and want to pay attention to their needs.

▶ **What do you want to know about me?**

Your employees are curious about you. They want to know whether or not you have a family, what your education and career history is, and what your hobbies are. How open you are will be reflected in how comfortable and open employees are with you. It will also affect the degree to which employees use you as a resource.

If you're currently working in technology but have a finance background, your employees won't know you have this outside expertise unless you share it with them. As a result, employees may not come to you when they have a finance question.

I ask all of my direct reports to share their education and career history with their teammates. And I repeat this activity every time a new person joins the team. This way, everyone is familiar with the entire team's areas of expertise and can ask for help with things that might be outside the scope of his or her current job.

I once worked for one of the most senior people in an organization. He talked incessantly about his kids, their high school basketball careers, and his fishing trips. It was well known in the office that you didn't dare get Mike talking about basketball or fishing unless you had an hour to spare. This was especially frustrating because Mike presented himself as always busy. There were weeks when I couldn't get on his calendar to meet with him, but if I swung by his office, stuck my head in, and asked how his son's basketball game went, I'd still be there an hour later. This inconsistency frustrated his employees, who were also busy and felt disrespected when he had time to talk about his son's game but not their projects.

The other extreme was Adam, one of Mike's colleagues who shared absolutely nothing personal with his employees. He believed in keeping his work and home life separate. As a result, Adam's direct reports knew absolutely nothing about him outside the office. They only knew he was married because he brought his wife to the company holiday party—seven months pregnant! His employees were shocked to discover he was married and about to have a baby. It was downright weird and made people wonder if they could trust him.

Strike a balance with your teams. Let them see the human part of you. Just don't share so much about your life that it becomes an inappropriate distraction.

▸ What additional questions do you have?

This is a more neutral question than "What concerns do you have?" It allows employees to ask whatever they would like, developing your relationship and the trust that you're working to engender. Let the employee know you're always available to him, will do your best to answer his questions, and will respond to requests and feedback.

I use the following language when completing an initial Candor Conversation™ and invite you to use it, or something like it:

> *"Thank you for having this conversation with me. I know it may have seemed a bit unusual and different from the initial conversations you've had with managers in the past. I know some of the questions I asked you were personal and we don't really know each other yet.*
>
> *"I am committed to your career and to your success and satisfaction in this organization. The more I know about you, the better I'll be able to assist you and provide you with what you need to be successful.*
>
> *"I want you to feel free to call on me anytime during our working relationship and to speak candidly with me. And when I become busy or stressed and am not available enough, please find a way to tell me.*
>
> *"I'm excited to have you on my team, and I know that you're going to do great things."*

This is, of course, my language. You'll want to use your own. Just be sure to complete the conversation in some way that makes the employee feel valued and respected (as opposed to poked and prodded), which reiterates the purpose of the discussion.

A STRONG START
ON-BOARDING EMPLOYEES POWERFULLY

Provide your employees with background information about their role, your role, the department, and the team. This is another "basic" that's rarely, if ever, covered. Provide context.

It's a little like prepping a friend before he comes to your house for dinner for the first time. *"My dad can't hear out of his left ear, so make sure you always speak into the right one. Aunt Mable lost her son in a skydiving accident, so don't mention that that's your favorite hobby. And Uncle Al is a die-hard Mets fan, so don't mention the Yankees if you want dessert."* You get the point.

New employees don't know the history, politics, or "how things work" at a company. To some extent, that's good. You want new employees to create their own impressions without tainting them with yours. That said, knowing some history will help employees have a strong start. And conversely, it's important to introduce new employees to the team, share the new employee's background and areas of expertise, and explain what he was hired to do.

▶ A True-Life Scenario

At one organization, my new boss met with me on my first day but didn't give me any history about my department or my role. Nor did she tell my teammates what I had been hired to accomplish. I wasn't aware of the importance of these omissions until much later.

During my first few weeks on the job, I went on my merry way, doing what I was hired to do. Within a few weeks, it was clear that one of my colleagues, a fellow manager, didn't like me. In fact, I was pretty sure she hated me. I had no idea why. I was as nice to her as I could be. I went out of my way to be friendly, to get to know her, and to learn about her role.

Leaving a meeting one day, she was clearly furious. And in the hallway she let me have it. She yelled, "Just who the hell do you think you are coming in here and—!" Every action she questioned was exactly what I had been hired to do.

Later I found out this manager had been asking for several years to do the work I was hired to do but was not seen as the right fit. In the absence of a permanent person in the role, she had been permitted to do some of the work in a part-time capacity. She was, however, never seen as a viable candidate. And the worst thing was that despite working for the company for eighteen years, no one had told her she wasn't a good fit for the job and would never be considered for it.

As in many companies, no one gave my peer clear and direct feedback. No one told my new team why I had been hired and what I was there to accomplish—a typical but unfortunate and distressing scenario. My colleague was threatened by me, upset, and verbal about it. She did the best she could to sabotage my every effort and my reputation the entire time I was with the company. Had I not been transferred to the company headquarters in a different part of the country, I believe she would have successfully run me out of the organization.

Much of this confusion and anger could have been easily avoided. If my colleague had been told the truth about her perceived limitations and future with the company, or lack thereof, she could have made an informed career choice about whether to stay or go. Had her inappropriate behavior been managed, I would not have felt uncomfortable going to work. Had I known the history, I would have treaded a bit more lightly around her and perhaps looked for more opportunities for us to work together.

Don't underestimate the importance of providing context both for existing and new employees when on-boarding a new employee. Remember, give people more information than you think you need to.

> Human beings have a need to know. When we don't know what's happening and why, we make things up and talk about them to whoever will listen.

EFFECTIVE MANAGERS **ASK FOR FEEDBACK**

Your direct reports can work hard on your behalf or they can do their minimal best. Managers who earn employees' loyalty periodically ask for and are open to feedback.

Consider asking your employees one or two of the following questions:

- ▸ What is working for you about my management style?
- ▸ What do you wish I would do more?

▶ What would you like me to start, stop, and continue doing?

These are perfect questions to ask during performance appraisals, goal reviews, and regular one-on-one meetings. Each meeting with an employee should be a dialogue rather than a managerial lecture, with the employee nodding and attempting to absorb the information (a.k.a., pretending to listen while secretly killing you off). Both the manager and the direct report have a right to make requests and communicate when their expectations are not met.

One reason to ask employees for feedback is that few managers do it. When you do what others don't, you set yourself apart, demonstrating that you care about your employees in ways previous managers have not. When employees receive calls from headhunters or are tempted to go work for competitors for more money, they'll have to weigh the risk of leaving a caring and interested manager who asks for input about what the employee wants and needs to succeed and who tries to meet those needs. These are very unusual things for a manager to do—anyone who has had more than one job knows this. So while your fresh-out-of-school twenty-somethings may not know how good they have it with you, your more seasoned employees will. If they're smart, your employees will be hesitant to leave such an unusually reciprocal relationship.

If the idea that employees have the right to make requests and provide you with feedback is in conflict with your own beliefs or experience, consider this—the alternative doesn't work. People don't want to be told what to do but never asked for input. Employees don't want to work for people with whom they can't speak candidly or make requests.

Remember, people leave managers, not jobs. If employees don't like working for you, what's to prevent them from going elsewhere? Asking for input and feedback is one of the keys to having productive, satisfied employees who will be loyal to you and your organization.

SUMMARY: *THE BETTER YOU KNOW YOUR EMPLOYEES, THE EASIER THEY ARE TO MANAGE.*

The ultimate purpose of all these questions is to eliminate the guessing that's inherent in managing people. Learning more about your employees from the onset of your working relationship allows you to give them opportunities that motivate long-term performance. You're creating an open relationship in which employees can make requests and be honest without fear of recourse.

If you ask the questions consistently, you'll never again be surprised by an employee who becomes frustrated or disengaged or who resigns. Instead, you'll have more power and control in all your managerial relationships.

CHAPTER 5

MANAGING UP
WITH CANDOR

Your relationship with your direct supervisor is one of the most, if not *the* most, important relationships you have at work. Your boss is a conduit to interesting work, organizational exposure, and good pay increases. Without these things, jobs become less fulfilling and short-lived. Your boss is, of course, responsible for managing you. But savvy employees know that they also manage their bosses. When we don't manage upward, our careers stagnate.

We have all been caught off guard by unexpected feedback during a performance appraisal. Or we've worked until 11:00 p.m. trying to get something done that, we later find out, our manager didn't look at for three weeks. At some point, you'll be frustrated with every manager. But that frustration can be mitigated by asking more questions and getting more information at the onset of jobs and projects. The more information employees have about their boss's preferences and how the organization functions, the better employees' work experiences will be. In addition to the questions listed in chapters three and four, consider asking your boss some of the questions listed throughout this chapter.

▸ **What specific aspects of a project would you like me to communicate to you? In what format and how frequently do you want that information communicated?**

Have you ever worked on a project, thinking you were doing exactly what your manager wanted, only to find out she had a specific picture of how the work should look, and it was nothing like what you provided? We often learn the hard way about how people like to receive information.

ASK FOR FEEDBACK ALONG THE WAY

Most of us have also worked for a manager who approved a work in process, but who, when the final product was completed, rejected it and told us to make significant changes or start over. This is the type of frustration that leads employees to create voodoo dolls of their managers.

Everyone has a preference regarding communication of information—how much, in what format, and how often. Even people who say they don't care usually have a preference. These are the people who have no opinion about where you go out to eat—until you choose a place they don't like. Some managers want to know exactly what you're working on at all times. Others are happy to receive periodic updates on just the big initiatives.

Why guess what your boss is expecting, when it's such an easy question to ask?

At any point in a working relationship or project, you can ask your manager or project leader how often she wants to receive updates, in what way, and with what level of detail. If your manager tells you she doesn't care to be updated on progress of the current project, ask for feedback on work you've done in the past.

Consider asking:

▸ **Did my last update contain enough detail, or would you have liked more information?**

> ▸ **What can I change about how I put the data together to make it easier to review?**

> ▸ **Would you like to see the data in bullet format or in paragraphs? Or in charts, graphs, or tables?**

My advice is to check in and get feedback regularly on a work in process. If your manager tells you she doesn't need to see the work until it's complete, be candid by telling her, *"I want to work efficiently. Your feedback on my progress will ensure I'm going in the right direction."*

Perhaps remind your manager of a past project that disappointed her, requiring additional work. *"I want to give you what you're looking for the first time. Remember the Baker project? The data I provided wasn't quite what you wanted, and it wasn't in the right format. If I can get it right the first time, I'll be able to move on to the next project more quickly."*

YOUR JOB IS TO MAKE YOUR BOSS **LOOK GOOD**

The higher someone gets in management, the more his performance is evaluated based on his team's performance. This is why smart managers surround themselves with the best people. The most senior person in an organization divides the organization's goals among his direct reports. His direct reports then disseminate their goals to their employees. When organizations are aligned, your annual goals are ultimately a portion of your manager's goals.

Thus, regardless of what you think of your boss, your job is to make him or her look good. And the more clearly you understand how your boss is being measured, the better position you are in to achieve your own goals.

> ▸ **What are your goals for the department?**

> ▸ **How does our department fit into the organization's strategic plan and annual goals?**

Knowing where your boss sees your department going helps ensure that your actions are aligned with his vision and focused on what's most important. It also gives you insight into where the organization is going as a whole. Knowing the big picture puts each job in context and highlights its importance.

In large organizations, it's easy to feel like a nonessential cog in a big, impersonal machine. This is where the "it's not my job" syndrome comes from. Employees who are aware of the company's vision and strategic direction are more likely to see how their roles contribute to the execution of that vision and are more likely to remain engaged.

▸ **What do I need to achieve in the next 30, 60, and 90 days?**

Most driven professionals have had a day, or one hundred days, when they decided they wanted their evenings and weekends back and were tired of sleeping with their BlackBerrys. I don't doubt that these Type As are working hard. I just wonder whether they are consistently working on the things their boss thinks are most important.

Here's an example: A few months ago, a manager I coach was feeling overwhelmed. Her job had grown, and she didn't know how to balance all of her responsibilities. She was working a lot of hours and was worried that she was failing and that something important would fall through the cracks.

I suggested she make a list of everything she did, take it to her next meeting with her boss, and ask for his help prioritizing her responsibilities. I suggested she ask him to put an A next to the initiatives he viewed as a top priority, a B by the next most important responsibilities, and a C next to the least important items.

She learned a lot during that conversation. Some of the things she felt were important and was spending an exorbitant amount of time on were not as important to her boss. She relaxed and focused on what was most important to her boss. And her boss retained an employee who was quickly becoming a turnover risk.

Another example: A client told me about a weekly ninety-minute meeting she attended. Each week the meeting facilitator sent multiple documents two minutes before the meeting began and expected attendees to have reviewed them. The meetings always began ten minutes late, and the facilitator answered her cell phone during meetings.

After a few months, my client was beyond exasperated and told her boss she no longer wanted to attend the meetings. He looked surprised, told her she never needed to attend, and asked why she'd been going in the first place. If only she'd communicated with her boss before attending her first meeting, she could have made better use of her time.

What you think is important may not be what your manager thinks is important. Work on agreed-upon priorities to avoid major frustration later.

ASK HOW YOU'RE BEING **EVALUATED**

Professional athletes would never get on the court or field if they didn't know the rules of the game, and you shouldn't either. If you don't know how your performance is being measured and what a good job looks like, you might meet your manager's expectations and, then again, you might not.

▶ **How will we track and measure success?**

Your manager should work with you to establish annual goals. If she doesn't, write down your own targets and metrics and bring them to her for review and approval. Bring the goals to your regular meetings with her and review their status, making changes throughout the year if organizational priorities change. If you don't work from specific, measurable, and agreed-upon goals, it's likely that your year-end performance appraisal will be subjective and upsetting.

Take your performance into your own hands and work from agreed-upon goals, regardless of the company's policy on goal setting and evaluating performance.

LEARN ABOUT **THE PAST**

While you should form your own impressions when starting a new job, it's helpful to know a little about the situation you're walking into. If the person you are replacing was widely loved, you may have a bit of a challenge being embraced by your new coworkers. If she was widely loathed, you will probably be a breath of fresh air. In either case, you will have to overcome whatever feelings people have about what your role can or can't provide. You will have to sell not only yourself but also how much benefit your role can bring to the organization. Knowing the history from the beginning may alter your approach. Consider saying:

▸ **Tell me about the person I'm replacing. If the role is new, why was the job created?**

If you're an assertive, get-it-done type, and the person you're replacing was known for being aggressive, you might take a softer approach than you otherwise would. If your predecessor was not assertive and people doubted his ability because of his quiet style, you might start off a little more strongly than you otherwise would have.

If your job is a new role in the organization, it's also important to know why the job was created. Salaries are an organization's greatest cost, and jobs are created only when there is a significant, perceived need. What happened that made the company choose to fill the job now rather than a year ago or six months from now? Just as with establishing clear goals and metrics, knowing how your role fits into the organization's strategic direction must determine where you put your time and budget dollars.

If your position is not a new role, it's useful to know why your predecessor left. If she left to move to another state to be closer to her family, great. If she left because it was a struggle to get things done, it's useful to know that so you can avoid the same pitfalls. Perhaps she was frustrated with the people, politics, or resources. This knowledge may alter your expectations of what you can get done quickly and help you modify your approach to people and projects. While you should form your own opinions, it's always good to know what you're walking into.

▶ **What type of work/projects would you like me to be responsible for?**

▶ **What type of work would you rather I avoid?**

The person you report to may have, in the not-too-distant past, done the work you were hired to do. And she may still have an interest in doing some of that work herself. Everyone has her pet projects, areas of passion, and favorite things to do. Identifying the parts of your job that your manager really wants to do herself or wants to be heavily involved with will reduce redundant work and the potential for your feeling micromanaged.

When you know up front that your boss has a great deal of passion for a certain project, you can involve her more than you otherwise would. You'll also be less likely to take her desire to be involved as feedback that you are not doing your job. You'll know she's asking for details from a genuine interest in the work, not because she doesn't trust you.

Here's a perfect example: One of my clients, Lauren, decided her department needed to create a website for their external customers. She delegated the project to Lindsey, one of her direct reports, who was a good writer and project manager. Lindsey was perfect for this project. Despite trusting Lindsey, Lauren stayed involved in the website design, oversaw the vendor who created the site, reviewed all the artwork, and wrote the website's content.

It wasn't until Lindsey stopped making decisions that Lauren recognized that she had become over involved with the website. When Lauren asked why Lindsey was waiting to make decisions,

Lindsey told her, "You're going to change what I do anyway, so I may as well let you make the decisions."

Lauren liked website design. Her passion for the work made it difficult for her to step back and let Lindsey do her job.

Had Lindsey asked up front how Lauren wanted to be involved, Lindsey would have known that Lauren's overinvolvement was not a reflection of her competence. Rather, it was a demonstration of Lauren's interest in marketing.

LEARN THE ORGANIZATION'S POLITICS AND UNWRITTEN RULES

It's helpful to know the history of the team you're joining. As my story in the last chapter illustrated, had I known my teammate who called me out at every opportunity and for no apparent reason wanted my job, I would have approached the relationship very differently.

▸ **What should I know about the team culture?**

▸ **Does the department have history that I should know?**

▸ **What is the team's understanding of my role and how do they feel about it?**

Several years ago I was offered a job leading a department that had just lost a very damaging manager. The previous manager had made changes without much rationale, reprimanded people for no apparent reason, and questioned every action her direct reports took. She managed by intimidation, and the result was 50 percent turnover in fewer than six months. As is typical, the most talented and driven employees got other jobs and left the company. The employees who remained were less marketable and weaker performers.

I was an internal candidate for the position and knew the department's history. My first question was whether I was permitted to fire the employees who didn't perform and pick my own team. I got a resounding "no" in response. I would inherit the existing team members and would not be permitted to make staffing changes. I knew I couldn't be successful with the employees who remained, and I turned down the job. Had I not asked for that information during the interview process, I would have accepted the job and been the next person to leave.

On the flip side, had I accepted the job, I would have walked into a group of scared and disenfranchised employees. My natural leadership style of quick action and direct communication would have fallen flat. But if I hadn't known the department's history, I wouldn't have known to alter my approach. Instead, I would have further alienated my new direct reports and never understood why they resisted every change I made.

▸ **Who should I meet in the organization?**

▸ **Whose meetings should I attend?**

Learning a new organization takes time. New employees coming in from the outside know how to do the work they were hired to do but not necessarily how to get it done in this particular organization. How are decisions made? Who holds the power? Who is important to build a relationship with, and who is less important?

It may sound political to say that not everyone in the organization is important to your success, but quite frankly, it's true. The sooner you learn who you need and who needs you, the sooner you can invest in the relationships that matter most.

Create a focused start at your new position by asking who you need to meet and whose meetings you need to attend. Ask your boss for introductions to pivotal people.

▸ **What's the best time to take a vacation?**

▸ **When should I never take a vacation?**

Many employees ask for days off not knowing that the time they've scheduled for a vacation is the worst time of year to be away. Managers know the organization so well they forget that new employees don't. It doesn't occur to managers to tell new employees the dates or times of the year they absolutely must be in the office. But managers will question an employee's judgment if she inadvertently requests those days off.

> **What other questions do you have? What else would you like to know about me?**

These questions show you are open and want to share information about yourself.

> **I'm always working on improving my performance. Is it okay if I periodically check in and ask for feedback?**

Despite the best of intentions, many managers don't give enough feedback. They may be too busy or uncomfortable to give feedback, or perhaps they lack a proper sense of an employee's performance to give meaningful feedback.

If you work long enough, you'll have a manager who doesn't give a lot of feedback. Rather than being frustrated, just ask for it, having gotten permission up front to do so. Asking for feedback when the relationship begins sets the expectation, and it helps you to avoid giving your manager the impression that you're asking for feedback because she isn't doing her job or because you think there is something wrong (even if that's the case).

> **You can find additional questions to ask your direct supervisor at:**
> www.leadershipandsalestraining.com/sayanything

SUMMARY: *ASK WHAT YOUR MANAGER EXPECTS; DON'T WAIT TO BE TOLD.*

You are responsible for your career—no one else is. During your career you'll have managers who set expectations and give feedback, and you'll have those who don't. If you haven't had a bad manager yet, just wait. He or she is coming.

Your job satisfaction and performance can't be dependent on the person you work for. Don't wait to be told what's important to your boss or how to approach new relationships. Likewise, don't assume that you're doing a good job just because no one has told you otherwise.

Asking any or all of the questions covered in this chapter gives you more control over your performance, reputation, and business relationships. Don't let work happen to you. Take control. Doing so demonstrates that you're committed to doing a great job, and it gets your relationship with your new manager off to a powerful start.

CHAPTER 6

STRENGTHENING
INTERNAL BUSINESS
RELATIONSHIPS

I f you're following the relationship-building practices in this book, you've told your coworkers and the people you support internally that you want a good relationship with them. You've requested feedback and promised to say thank you when you get it. And you've asked about working-style preferences—email versus voicemail, phone versus in-person meetings, etc.—so you don't unnecessarily and unknowingly annoy people and damage relationships. The next step is to learn more about what the people and departments you work with do on a daily basis, the challenges they face, and how your work impacts theirs.

DEPARTMENTS **DON'T** TALK TO EACH OTHER

In my experience, most people in organizations know very little about what other departments do beyond the basics. We often don't know what types of challenges and constraints other departments deal with. And even less often do we know why other departments require certain forms, time lines, and processes. Asking these questions helps people get their jobs done and eliminates much of the strife, redundant work, and frustration that is prevalent in most workplaces.

Here's an example: About seven years ago, when I led an operations division, I was sitting in a meeting with multiple department heads. The purpose of the meeting was to ensure that each department knew the big projects and initiatives that other departments were working on. Each leader had five minutes to talk about the work his or her group was doing. When the conversation turned to marketing, the VP of marketing described a project his team was working on. Unfortunately, my team had been working on that same thing for months.

I was immediately frustrated. I ran a lean department. Why hadn't someone in marketing told me they were working on this? We could have pooled our efforts, or I could have pulled out and focused my staff on other things. I was furious. As I thought about it more, I realized that I hadn't informed anyone in marketing about the work my department was doing either.

This double work, rework, and lack of communication is not unusual in organizations. In fact, it's the norm. Mid-project one department discovers another department has been working—for months, if not years—on the very same things.

The ensuing conversation goes something like this: "I wish we had known you were working on this. We could have worked together. What a waste of resources. We really need to work on the communication in this organization."

THINGS BECOME PERSONAL
WHEN THERE IS **NO PROCESS**

Every department has its own way of doing things. There is a reason why payroll needs to be reported by three o'clock, why you must supply accounts payable with a $2.00 receipt for a cup of coffee when the federal government doesn't require it, and why you have to go through purchasing for some purchases but not others.

For the most part, there is a good reason—at least in someone's opinion—for those practices.

Unfortunately, there is often little communication about these policies and procedures. We just expect people to know why we do what we do and to follow our rules. When other departments don't play along, we become annoyed, grumbling about how difficult they are to work with and how they make our lives hard. At the same time, the offending department is complaining about your stupid rules and how inflexible you are.

Organizations often call me to mediate disputes between people and departments, and to help people work better together. Here's a typical scenario: A policy or procedure wasn't clear to one department, so they ignored it. The other department took this disregard for their policies personally and felt affronted. The two departments began to hate each other and each team decided the other team was difficult to work with and incompetent.

When I dig into these situations, I usually discover that issues that appear personal typically start with a lack of process or a lack of clarity about another department's way of doing things. Creating a process or explaining the rationale for an existing process, and coming to an agreement of what each team will do going forward, typically shifts the relationship.

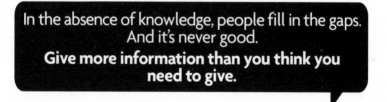

In the absence of knowledge, people fill in the gaps. And it's never good.
Give more information than you think you need to give.

For the most part, people will do what you ask, but they want to know why you're asking. They need to understand the rationale behind what they're being asked to do. Once they understand, they often stop complaining and follow the rules.

I'll keep my receipts for items under $25.00—but I want to know why it's required. I'll go through purchasing even though it may be more expensive—but I want to know why. I'll stop working on a project that was a top priority yesterday—but I want to know why the priorities changed.

TREAT YOUR COWORKERS LIKE CUSTOMERS

When he started his new job, the vice president of IT at my last organization wisely met with each department leader to learn about our needs and to educate us how to best utilize his department. He told us what IT was positioned to do, how to work with his employees to get what we needed, and how to get into their work flow. In fifteen years of working in organizations, this VP of IT was the only leader who reached out to me, like a consultant, to learn about my department and how he could best meet my needs.

Why don't more people do as that IT department head did, introducing themselves to new colleagues, learning about each department, and educating people how to best work with them? I suspect it simply never occurs to them. Treat your internal customers just like you treat your external customers. You have to earn everyone's business. Just because someone is *supposed* to work with you doesn't mean that he will.

Just as with asking about working-style preferences, asking other departments about their goals and how teams can work well together is extremely unusual. Asking these questions is another way to differentiate yourself and to improve your working relationships and your professional reputation.

I always suggest that individuals and teams who rely on each other to get their work done regularly get together to talk about what each team does, how they do it, and why. For example, the person who leads your department should reach out to the finance department to find out what kinds of reports they need and by when. She should seek out accounts payable staff to learn the right way to submit expense reports, so her employees are reimbursed in a timely way. She should meet with the head of purchasing to be sure her team doesn't violate policies, which many people unknowingly do.

Schedule a meeting with each department you support and rely on in order to get your job done. Let each person you meet with know you want to learn more about her business so you can meet her needs. Your job during the meeting is to ask questions and listen, not talk about your department or yourself. When you kick off the conversation, reiterate the purpose of the meeting. All team members can attend these discussions, or one person from each team can meet and report back to the rest of the team.

Asking the following questions will help you learn the objectives, challenges, and needs of the departments you support or that support you. Ask the questions that feel most important at this time. Don't ask all of them; this could potentially overwhelm your colleagues. After all, you can always meet again.

QUESTIONS TO ASK **DEPARTMENT LEADERS** YOU SUPPORT OR WHO SUPPORT YOU

1. What is your department best known for? What do you want to be known for?

2. Tell me about your department's business goals. What do the next few years look like? What are you working on this year?

3. What's the most important thing your department will accomplish this year?

4. What deadlines, rules, and regulations impact your business and activities?

5. What causes you frustration?

6. What keeps you up at night? What are you concerned about?

7. How does my department's work impact your department?

8. On what type of work does it make sense for us/our departments to work together?

9. What would I or my department do that would cause you difficulties and make your life harder?

10. What would make me and my department easy to work with?

11. Can I come to your team meetings?

12. Can I do a short presentation for your staff about the work we do?

13. What do you want to know about me or my department?

14. What else should I know about you and your department?

The last piece of this conversation is letting your colleagues know that you'd like to check in with them periodically to assess how things are going and then asking for permission to do so. I call this check-in a Relationship Inventory™ and suggest you do it quarterly. The next chapter will lay out exactly how to conduct a Relationship Inventory.

Asking about working-style preferences and learning more about your colleagues' goals and concerns helps you focus on the right work, and it makes you a good business partner. But this is not a one-time conversation. As in all relationships, revisiting expectations and asking for feedback is an ongoing process. Check in periodically to assess what's changed in your colleagues' department since you last spoke. Then ask whether you and your department are meeting their expectations.

The conversation could go something like this:

"Our department's practice is to get in touch at least once a quarter to make sure you're getting everything you need. Is it okay if I reach

*out to you a few times a year to get some feedback? If yes, how would
you like me to do that? Is it okay if I call you?"*

Each department head will say yes. Even if she doesn't want
to say yes, she will. But set the expectation that you will check in
regularly only if you intend to do so. To tell someone you're going
to ask for input and then to never do so is worse than saying nothing at all. Set alarms in whatever calendaring system you're using,
and then make that call when the reminder comes up.

Asking other departments about their goals, concerns, and
deadlines serves many purposes. It will make your job easier. You
will know what people need from you and why—you won't have
to guess. And the people you depend on will know what you need
from them, which makes it more likely that your needs will be met.

BE SOMEONE PEOPLE **WANT TO WORK WITH**

Regardless of company protocol, people work with the people
they want to work with and avoid the ones they don't. If you call
IT for help and the desktop support specialist likes you, he will
come to your desk first, regardless of where you fall in his ticket
list that day. And while this may not be fair, we all know it's the way
things work. There are certain people whose names we're happy to
see show up on our phones and certain people we let go to voicemail, because we just can't deal with them today.

People can work with you, around you, and against you. I want
people to enjoy working with you. The more people want to work
with you, the easier and more enjoyable your job will be.

One way to ensure people want to work with you is to learn
more about their business so that you are a help, not a hindrance.
When you make people's lives easier, they will make your life easier.
When you follow others' rules, they are more likely to follow yours.
Quid pro quo is alive and well, despite what your company hand-
book says.

Asking policy and procedure questions at the beginning of working relationships helps avoid missteps, wasted time, and frustration for all concerned. Other department leaders should come to you, ask what you need, and inform you of the guidelines for working with them. But most won't. Take the initiative to have this conversation. It makes everyone's life easier, especially yours.

You may be thinking, *"I've been working with the same people for years. If I go and ask how my department impacts theirs, they're going to think I'm an idiot and will wonder what I've been doing all these years."*

But that's simply not the case.

If you've never asked your colleagues these questions, they know that! They know that you don't know. And they are struggling with the same things you are—employees who incorrectly fill out expense reimbursement forms, teams that spend time on work other departments are doing, and employees who complain how difficult other departments are to work with. Fellow leaders and colleagues want and need to have these conversations with you— even if they haven't articulated it.

Get additional questions to ask your internal customers at:
www.leadershipandsalestraining.com/sayanything

SUMMARY: *TREAT EVERYONE YOU WORK WITH AS A CUSTOMER.*

Much of the strife, redundant work, and lack of communication in organizations is predictable—and avoidable. Don't assume the people you work with know what you do and why. Likewise, don't assume you know your coworkers' priorities. Make appointments with the people you work with most closely and ask what they're working on this year. Ask how you and they can work together and make each other's lives easier. Everyone appreciates being asked about their priorities and how you can work together.

Asking these questions is an easy way to differentiate yourself and become someone others want to work with.

CHAPTER 7

RELATIONSHIPS REQUIRE
MAINTENANCE

Once you've established relationships with your colleagues, it's easy to feel you've earned the right to coast a little. You've already done what almost no one ever does—asked a lot of questions at the beginning of the relationship. But now you've been working with these people for years. You know what your boss, coworkers, and direct reports need and how they need it. And of course, if you're doing something that doesn't work, they'll tell you, right? Wrong.

Starting a relationship by asking what people expect from you, but never checking in to ask how things are going, is like taking someone's order in a restaurant but never checking back to see how he is enjoying his meal. If the food isn't quite right, the customer is forced to track down his server to make a request. But most people are not likely to do that. They are more likely to leave a lousy tip and tell everyone they know how bad the service was. Your coworkers are no different. They're more likely to work around you than tell you they're dissatisfied.

The priorities of a business tend to change. What was important during the first quarter may not be a priority in the second. If you don't periodically check in and find out what's changed in your coworkers' departments, you could be dedicating time and resources in the wrong places and never know it.

Relationships are a dance and require practice and maintenance. The most frequent comment about marriage is that "it takes work." Business relationships are no different. Asking questions and setting expectations are not one-time events; these behaviors are ongoing elements of good relationships—personal and professional.

Determine what people need and assess how the relationship is going by watching and asking questions. Then adjust accordingly. If direct reports and coworkers need more assistance, you step in. If they need less help, you step out.

When people don't respond as we expect or don't respond at all, many of us spin our wheels trying to figure out what it is that people need. We wonder, *"Should I call him? Should I send an email? Maybe I should go to his office. I don't want to bug him. Maybe I'll wait."* We make ourselves crazy trying to figure out what others expect, and it's unnecessary.

As discussed throughout this book, don't guess—ask. Asking questions about working-style preferences kicks relationships off in a powerful way. Maintaining relationships over time requires asking for feedback and reminding people that you really want to hear what they have to say.

YOU CAN BE **FIRED** AND NEVER KNOW IT

A few weeks ago I got a call from Michelle, a manager at a large call center. She asked if I could do some train-the-trainer work with her customer service representatives, because their job responsibilities had recently changed. Rather than just answering customers' phone calls, her representatives were also going to be conducting new-hire customer service training.

I know Michelle's company well. They have a large customer service training department that is dedicated to new-hire training.

"What happened to the training department? Why is your team being asked to train new hires?" I asked.

Michelle told me that her boss, the director of the call center, was dissatisfied with the training department's work and had decided that Michelle's team, even with no training experience, could do a better job.

"This is very, very bad," I thought to myself. If I were leading the "former" training department and was in this situation, I'd either be job hunting or parking myself in that director's office to figure out what I needed to do to meet the department's needs.

The bottom line is that the training department got fired. And you can be fired too—either overtly, when you're asked to leave, or subtly, when people work around you.

Here is another example that I hope has never happened to you. The VP of marketing at a firm I used to work for got a call from a friend who had seen the VP's job posted on a job board. The friend said, "Hey, buddy, I just wanted to see if you were still there. Your job is posted on Monster, so I figured you'd moved on."

That's what I call feedback. It isn't specific or particularly helpful, but it is feedback.

In this case, the company determined that the VP of marketing wasn't working out and decided to replace him. To reduce the amount of time the job would be vacant and to keep the current VP engaged, the company began searching for his replacement before telling him that he wasn't meeting expectations.

This is wrong, but it happens all the time.

Here is a final example: One of my clients asked me to coach a director named Ann who was struggling with her interpersonal skills. One of Ann's direct reports, Sarah, went to Ann's boss and complained that Ann was condescending, played favorites, and didn't provide any value. Sarah then asked to report to a different manager. Ann got "fired" as a manager by her dissatisfied employee.

During my first meeting with Ann, I asked how she felt about Sarah, her direct report, asking for a different manager. Ann looked at me curiously. "What do you mean? Sarah and I have a good working relationship. She told me she felt we were too similar and thus thought she should have a different manager. I didn't question that."

This woman was living on a different planet. While I wanted to shake her and tell her to get off whatever medication she was on, I tried a different approach. I said, "Ann, when an employee asks for a different manager, it's a big deal. Sarah is giving you the opportunity to look at what you're doing and assess what is and isn't working. Sarah may feel that you were too similar, but I doubt it. Something about the relationship wasn't working for her, and the only way you can find out is to ask." It astounded me that this had not occurred to Ann.

If you want to control your career, you must identify your blind spots and know your reputation. The only way to find out is to ask.

Consider conducting what I call a Relationship Inventory—a method of touching base with the people you work with to see what's changed in their business since you last talked. It's also an opportunity to ask for feedback.

You can schedule a meeting to ask for an update and get feedback, or you can use an already-scheduled meeting. It doesn't matter how you get the information; it just matters that you ask for it and respond appropriately.

Here is an example of how to conduct a Relationship Inventory: I've been doing training and HR consulting for one of my clients, a professional services firm, for the past three years. The managing partner and I meet once a month to review the work I've done in the last thirty days and to talk about next steps.

The last time we met, midway through the meeting, I said, "Michael, it's been a while since I asked this: How is my work for the firm going? What feedback have you gotten? What requests do you have for me?"

It's as simple as that. You don't need to have a separate conversation from the one you were already having. Nor do you need an elaborate introduction. Just ask a few questions.

Questions to ask during Relationship Inventories are listed below. As I've advised for the other lists of questions provided throughout this book, ask a few questions during a conversation; don't recite the whole list. You want to have a conversation, not conduct an interrogation. You can always ask more questions during another conversation. As with the other lists, don't ask the questions via email or a written survey.

In addition to gathering information, remember that you're building rapport. Surveys provide great information and are efficient, but they don't strengthen relationships. There's a reason why companies bribe customers with free trips to Tahiti for filling out surveys. It's because no one wants to fill them out. Quite frankly, I'd rather pay to go to Tahiti than fill out their damn survey. Call or go see your colleagues in person to ask these questions.

You can open the Relationship Inventory conversation by saying something like this:

> *"Mike, thanks for making time to talk with me. I really appreciate it. Your feedback helps our department ensure we're focused on the right things. Please be candid. I want to hear whatever you have to say and I promise that I will say thank you. I may, at a later date, ask for additional information. But today I'm just going to listen."*

Then ask a few questions.

RELATIONSHIP INVENTORY QUESTIONS

1. What's happening in your department that you want me to know about?

2. What's changed in your business since we last met?

3. What's working about how our departments are working together?

4. What's not working about how our departments are working together?

5. How have we exceeded your expectations in the last few months?

6. How have we disappointed you in the last few months?

7. What's one change we could make that would make the biggest difference for you?

8. What's it like to work with the people who report to me?

9. What's most important for me to know?

"HOW IS IT GOING?" IS A GREETING, NOT A QUESTION

You'll notice that "How is it going?" is not one of the questions on the Relationship Inventory question list. The right answer to "How is it going?" is "Fine." And that is not helpful to you. You get what you ask for. If you ask a vague question, you'll get a vague answer. If you want useful information you can act upon, ask specific questions.

> **Watch the author demonstrate asking the questions at:**
> www.leadershipandsalestraining.com/sayanything

YOU WON'T DIE BY ASKING QUESTIONS

After reading the list of questions, some of you may be grabbing for your favorite kind of liquid courage, thinking there is no way you could ask them. I'm here to tell you that you can. You won't die. (Well, you will, but not from a conversation at work.) You can hear what people have to say. Because most people are afraid to say anything negative, they will most likely tread lightly. Choose candor over comfort. You can totally do this.

THE RIGHT ANSWER IS ALWAYS **"THANK YOU"**

You've already seen throughout this book that my recommended answer to feedback is "Thank you," even if you think the person has no idea what he is talking about and is dead wrong. How accurate he is doesn't matter. What matters is that you find out how you and your department are being perceived. Once you receive and digest that information, you can figure out how to respond. But during the initial conversation, "Thank you" is the right answer. We'll talk about what to say after "Thank you" later in this book.

SILENCE MAY BE GOLDEN AT A DAY CARE CENTER, BUT IT ISN'T HELPFUL AT WORK

We know most people are not candid and have a tendency to talk about people, not to them. Don't assume that because you haven't gotten any feedback from your boss that things are going well. Too many managers don't give *any* feedback—positive or negative.

Many employees are denied a promotion or a different internal job and are never told the reasons why. This lack of feedback doesn't give employees the necessary information to alter their behavior so they can become more viable candidates the next time. Many companies take the wimpy, cover-your-butt way out and eliminate positions instead of telling employees they're not performing.

Smart careerists don't wait to be told how they're doing at work—they ask. So don't assume your business relationships are going well and that you will automatically receive the feedback you need to do a great job and get ahead. Ask your internal customers, your coworkers, and your boss for feedback, and keep asking.

SETTING YOURSELF UP TO **WIN**

To sum up the last few chapters, creating working relationships that work—whether with your direct reports, supervisor, peers, or internal customers—requires setting expectations at the beginning of relationships and then asking for feedback regularly. The benefits of asking questions, ones that most people don't ask, are numerous:

▸ You form new relationships or strengthen existing relationships by building trust. People tend to trust those who take time to get to know them and honor their requests.

▸ You tell your colleagues you wanted a good relationship with them, one in which they feel comfortable providing feedback. Asking questions about working-style preferences demonstrates your commitment to creating and sustaining smooth working relationships.

▸ Knowing more about what other departments do and how you impact each other reduces redundant work and the frustration inherent in working in organizations.

▸ You differentiate yourself. When is the last time a coworker asked about your working-style preferences and how his department impacts yours? Asking that question is very rare—and the people who do it stand out. If you're one of them, you'll be perceived as proactive and easy to work with.

▸ When you know how people like to work, you can communicate in the way they prefer and make working relationships much smoother. Office drama and gossip will go down. Productivity and the degree to which you enjoy your job and working relationships will go up.

SUMMARY: *CHECK IN WITH YOUR INTERNAL CUSTOMERS EVERY QUARTER; ASK FOR FEEDBACK.*

Kicking off relationships by telling people you want a good relationship and asking about working-style preferences is a great start, but it's just the beginning. Relationships require maintenance. Check in with your coworkers quarterly and ask how their business has changed.

What are they working on now that they weren't focused on when you last met? What else has changed? What's gone well about the service you and your department have provided? How is your working relationship going? Assuming the status quo at work is a little like buying a new car, never changing the oil, and then being surprised when it dies when you hit 75,000 miles.

Instead, follow up. Ask for feedback, accept it graciously, and watch your business relationships and results improve.

CHAPTER 8

CAN I **TRUST** YOU?

You can tell your colleagues, your boss, and your direct reports that you want a good working relationship with them. You can ask for feedback and promise to say thank you. And you can ask about their working-style preferences. But none of this will make a difference if the people you work with don't trust you.

You have to demonstrate that you meant what you said and that you really are the person you say you are.

We all want to work with people we trust. Have you ever gotten feedback from someone you didn't really know, trust, or perhaps even like? How did you take it? Did that little voice in your head start fuming, *"Just who does he think he is? This guy comes in at 10:00 a.m., takes a two-hour lunch, and is gone by 4:30. And he knows nothing about my job. He should butt out and stick to things he knows something about."*

Or, *"She just doesn't like me. It wouldn't matter how good or bad my work was. Her reaction would be the same."*

We've all received feedback or input that we've questioned or invalidated because of our relationship, or lack thereof, with its source. If you want others to hear your suggestions and take them as you intend them, you must have trust-based relationships. If you don't, every word you say will be questioned and tested.

TRUST IS EARNED, **NOT AWARDED**

If you manage people, you have the right by your status and formal authority to deliver any sort of feedback you wish. The trouble is, no matter how senior your status and title, the rules about trust continue to apply. If the people you manage don't trust you, it will be difficult to deliver tough feedback to them. Your direct reports will question the validity of what you're saying and why you're saying it. Conversations will be longer and more emotional than necessary, and thus you'll probably avoid them and put off giving feedback until the right moment has long passed.

As relationships develop, it's important not to kill them by damaging trust. Building trust takes time. Breaking trust can happen in a moment. Do your best to avoid the behaviors that are classic trust and relationship killers.

RELATIONSHIP KILLER NUMBER ONE: **GOSSIP**

People have a tendency to talk about us, not to us. If you haven't been gossiped about, you just need to get out and meet more people.

If you have something to say, say it directly to the person involved. If you're not going to speak to the person directly, say nothing at all. As we all know, this is easier said than done.

Gossip will destroy relationships, organizational cultures, and careers faster than anything else. And we are all tempted to gossip.

LET'S **DEFINE** GOSSIP

Most of us consider gossip to be saying something bad about someone else when that person isn't there. But what if we say something good? *"Suzanne looked great last night. I think she's lost a lot of weight."* Is that also gossip?

Let's see how a dictionary defines *gossip*. According to Roget, *gossip* is "idle talk or rumor, especially about the personal or private affairs of others." Some synonyms for *one who gossips* are "chatterer," "talker," "gabbler," "rumormonger," "blabbermouth," "busybody," "chatterbox," "circulator," "gossipmonger," "informer," "meddler," "newsmonger," "parrot," "prattler," "snoop," "talebearer," "tattler," and "telltale gossip."

We're talking about managing your career, relationships, and reputation. I don't know about you, but I don't want to be known as a busybody or a blabbermouth who meddles in other people's business.

The strictest definition of gossip is talking about another person while she is not present. But for our purposes, let's say gossip is talking about another person so as to alter how others think about that person.

A few years ago I took a yearlong class with about eighty other people. The class met one weekend a quarter over twelve months and had a few ground rules, one of which was no gossip. Participants couldn't gossip anywhere, at any time, during the class's entire duration. No gossip with friends, family, or coworkers for a year.

When the class started, I assumed the no-gossip guideline would be no problem for me. Then I started to notice my behavior. At the time, I was a director in my organization and had one friend at work who was my typical confidant. Most of us have "our person" at work—someone we confide in and complain to. The two of us would sit in my office with the door closed, talking about all the bad decisions the leaders of our company had made. The moment I began paying attention to the no-gossiping rule, I realized that not only did I gossip, but I was good at it and even enjoyed it. (Oh, come on, admit it—it's fun.)

The problem is that gossiping breaks trust. If a coworker gossips with you about someone else, he will talk about you to someone else. You are not special or different. (Well, you are, but you know what I mean.) You are not exempt.

As you rise in an organization, you have exposure to more and more sensitive information. You know about employees' performance ratings, the organization's financial results, and impending layoffs. One criterion of promotion is being able to be trusted with sensitive information. If the senior people in your organization think you're a gossip and can't be trusted to keep confidences, your career is going nowhere.

People will never stop gossiping. It's one of those human things. We all do it, and we aren't going to quit. The best we can hope for is to reduce the amount of time we spend talking about other people behind their backs.

Gossip is most prevalent in families. A few weeks ago one of my friends was telling me about the grapevine that runs through her family. My friend has distant cousins she never talks to; she hasn't seen or spoken to these cousins in years. Yet from her mom's updates, my friend knows whose kids are failing in school, whose marriages are on the rocks, and who isn't speaking to whom. Her mom doesn't consider any of this information gossip. Rather, she thinks she's just keeping her daughter in the loop. That's nonsense. It's all gossip. My friend doesn't have a relationship with any of those people and yet she knows who is getting divorced and whose kids shoplift.

ORGANIZATIONS AREN'T TOO DIFFERENT FROM FAMILIES

I won't suggest you stop gossiping. I merely suggest you bring your coworkers' attention to the gossip circulating throughout your organization.

Whenever I work with organizations to improve their culture, I suggest they attempt to reduce the gossip that runs rampant in their conference rooms, break rooms, hallways, etc. I always get the same objection. "We're venting. That's different from gossiping. It makes us feel better."

That's not true.

I'll refer back to my situation and give you another example. One day, while my coworker and I were sitting in my office venting (gossiping) about a recent meeting, I realized how exhausting the conversation was. We were talking about all the things that frustrated us; as a result, we became more frustrated, not less.

Unless you're solving a problem or planning a conversation you know you need to have, your conversation is gossip. It will make you feel worse, not better.

If you do feel the need to talk about what's happening in your office, be sure to talk with someone either above you or at the same level. "Venting" with someone on a level below you is gossip and puts the other person in an awkward position. I'd prefer you take your conversation out of your office and tell your spouse, your friends outside of work (protecting the people you work with by changing their names, of course) or, better yet, your cat, who will never violate a confidence.

When people start to identify venting as gossip and begin to pay attention to how often they talk about people who aren't present, the gossip in your organization will be reduced.

One of the women in my yearlong class took on the no-gossip rule in her office. Megan didn't say anything or call anyone out. Rather, whenever she heard gossip, she would put two fingers in the air and wave the peace sign. Yes, I know, it's a little dorky. But she wanted a visual symbol that would draw attention to the gossip circulating in her office but that wasn't critical or judgmental. She wasn't calling anyone out. She was merely demonstrating her observation.

After a while the people in her office started asking what she was doing. "I'm taking a class that doesn't allow gossip. So whenever I hear gossip, I wave the peace sign," she explained.

Shortly thereafter, whenever Megan walked down the hall, things got very, very quiet. People saw her coming, noted they were gossiping, and stopped talking. Megan's coworkers reacted like drivers who spot a police car on the highway. All of a sudden there is a string of cars going the speed limit.

After a few weeks of Megan's waving of the peace sign, other people in Megan's office started doing it too. It was a small company of about 250 people, so word spread pretty fast. Soon the CEO approached her and asked what this peace sign thing was about. So Megan told him, "I'm taking a class and we're not allowed to gossip. So whenever I hear gossip, I wave the peace sign."

The CEO made it a company policy!

Notice where in your office people gossip. Each company has its spots—the break rooms, copy rooms, hallways, parking lots, happy hour, and, yes, even the bathrooms. Gentlemen, I know you don't do this. But here's a little education . . .

For women, the bathroom is a prime location for "the meeting after the meeting." Women walk into the bathroom after a meeting in which some new, stupid policy was announced, see their friends who were in the same meeting, and talk. But they check under the stalls first to make sure they're alone.

Women know men don't do this. Men are in and out, and no one had best speak to them in the men's room. But men have been wondering for years why women go to the bathroom in groups and are gone for twenty minutes. Well, now you know. We're talking about you.

RELATIONSHIP KILLER NUMBER TWO:
BREAKING YOUR WORD

Do the things you say you will do. Here's a goal to aspire to: Make only commitments you intend to keep. We all know this isn't possible, so do the next best thing. As soon as you realize you can't or won't keep a commitment, tell the people who are affected. Don't wait.

Do you know someone who is a "yes" person in life? Not a suck-up, but someone who is easily sold. Whenever an idea is presented—a company happy hour on Wednesday, tennis on Saturday, a hike on Sunday—this person gets excited and says, "Yes!"

These folks are the golden retrievers of scheduling. Everything sounds good in the moment. But when the day comes, they often don't want to do what they've committed to and they cancel.

You probably have people in your life who don't do what they say they will do. They say they're coming to your party but don't show. They agree to meet for lunch at noon and are consistently fifteen minutes late. They set a deadline for a project and then miss it. These people are unreliable and as a result are not trusted.

We all make agreements we can't keep. The key is not that you never break a commitment—it's to communicate that break as soon as you know. If you agreed on Monday to go to a weekend party and know on Wednesday that you can't make it, don't wait until the day of the event to tell the host. Most of us feel bad when we can't make an event that we committed to attend. So we wait and wait to cancel, but that just compounds the problem. If you commit to bring a salad to a friend's party or to give another guest a ride and later find you can't do it, sharing that information on Saturday is much more problematic than fessing up on Wednesday, when you realize you won't be going.

The same is true at work. If you've been delegated to do something you won't be able to accomplish by the established deadline, tell your boss or whomever you're accountable to for the work as soon as you know. Coming clean early will put you in a much more positive light than telling her the day of the deadline or, worse, after the deadline. The earlier your boss knows she needs a Plan B, the more options she has for getting the work done. It will not bode well for you to put her or anyone else in crisis mode.

RELATIONSHIP KILLER NUMBER THREE:
NOT TELLING THE TRUTH

We all do things we wish we hadn't done. We miss deadlines, make mistakes, and disappoint people. Adults are not very different from kids about confessing to failings. We've all said, "It wasn't me" or "I didn't do it" way beyond the age of nine. We don't want

to disappoint the people we work with. So sometimes when we get caught in a mistake, our gut reaction is to deny. And such denials always come back to bite us. Just fess up. If, in the moment, you get nervous and lie, quickly go back and tell the truth. The other person knows anyway. You're nailed either way. You might as well maintain your integrity and reputation as someone who tells the truth.

RELATIONSHIP KILLER NUMBER FOUR: WITHHOLDING INFORMATION

When people don't know what is happening or why, they make things up. This isn't malicious. It stems from a human need to know and understand what's happening in our surroundings. However, made-up information that starts quite innocently can quickly spread throughout an organization like a cancer, destroying the culture leaders are working to create.

For example, the word gets out that John, a longtime employee, is leaving the company. There has been no announcement that he is leaving, and anyone who knows this information has been told to keep it quiet. But a secret is only a secret when the person you told is dead. So, as with everything people are curious about, the word gets out.

The reason for John's departure has not been made public. But people have a "need to know" and thus they begin speculating. Perhaps John took a job with a competitor? Perhaps he had a fight with his boss and is leaving without another job? Maybe his wife got a job elsewhere and they're relocating? Or was John having an inappropriate relationship with one of his direct reports and so has been asked to leave? None of this is true, but that doesn't make any difference. Soon everyone "knows" one or more of these "explanations."

A little candor in the form of an organizational announcement would have mitigated the gossip and rumor mill. John and his direct report's integrity would be intact. People might be spending

time working rather than speculating. And the organization's leaders would have built goodwill for being candid and trusting that employees could handle sensitive information.

I'm not suggesting that managers tell their employees everything. There are some things that are not appropriate to share beyond executive teams. But the things leaders can't share are fewer than they think. For those of you who are not in a formal leadership role, ask more questions. The desire to understand what's behind policies and procedures demonstrates a willingness and interest in working well with people, which increases trust and strengthens relationships.

SUMMARY: *IF YOU WANT YOUR BUSINESS RELATIONSHIPS TO WORK, BUILD MORE TRUST.*

At the root of an organization's success and profitability is the quality of its relationships. All the communication skills and techniques in the world won't create smooth working relationships if people don't trust each other. Start to notice when you're gossiping. If you have something to say about someone, tell him directly or say nothing at all. When you realize you can't keep a commitment, let people know as soon as possible. If you make a mistake, admit it. And share more information than you think you can. Employees can handle the truth. The more you trust people, the more they will trust you.

CHAPTER 9

GIVING AND RECEIVING FEEDBACK—**WHAT, WHEN, WHY, AND HOW**

Think about the driving directions friends give to help you find their homes (well, directions they used to give before the introduction of Google Maps and in-car GPS systems). You're going to a friend's house for dinner. Since your hostess doesn't want you to get lost, she gives you detailed directions: "Go down Main, a street with lots of strip malls and fast-food places. After five miles the area becomes residential. After you pass three or four subdivisions, you'll see a museum on your left and a school on your right. Turn right at the school. If you see a hospital, you've gone too far."

You're driving and feel like you've gone farther than you were supposed to go. But you haven't seen the museum or the school. At this point you begin to doubt yourself and assume you've gone the wrong way, so you pull over and call your friend. She assures you that you're on the right track; you just haven't gone far enough. "Keep going and you'll see the school." And sure enough, a few minutes later, you see the school.

FEEDBACK IS OUR ROADMAP

Landmarks in driving directions serve as feedback, letting us know we're on the right track and are progressing toward our desired destination. Just as we need to know whether we're driving in the right direction, we need to hear both what's going well and what's not going well regarding our performance at work.

As difficult as most of us find it to deliver bad news, we address the good stuff even less frequently. We expect things to go well. We expect people to do what they say they will do and, for the most part, to deliver good work. Because we've come to expect these things to happen, we don't feel the need to acknowledge them when they do.

But positive feedback serves as a milestone, letting us know we're doing the right work and should keep doing what we're doing. If people don't know that what they're doing meets expectations, they're not likely to continue doing it. Why would they?

Consider this: You notice that one of your coworkers is really busy. She had a huge project assigned to her and is clearly overwhelmed. You offer to help and take some of her work home to complete at night and over the weekend. Thanks to the several extra hours you contributed, she delivers the project on time without wanting to jump out a window. But she never thanks you. How likely are you to help her again?

Here's another example: When I left my last job to start my training business, Jane, one of the women who had worked for me, got promoted. She was not permitted to add staff. So she took on my old role in addition to her existing responsibilities. Jane quickly became overwhelmed—she had too much to do and not enough time or resources to do it. Something had to give.

Like any good professional, Jane evaluated and prioritized everything she was doing. She decided which things were least important, the tasks she could either stop doing or put on the back burner. She chose to stop doing a series of reports she produced monthly that took several hours to complete and that no one ever commented on. It didn't take long for Brian, her boss, to come to her office, red-faced and frustrated, asking about the reports.

Jane didn't know that the reports were, in fact, a very big deal. They were the scorecard for her department and were reviewed by the CEO, CFO, and the two company owners every thirty days. Brian took for granted that Jane knew the reports were important; he didn't think he needed to mention how important it was for her to regularly complete and submit them. Both Jane and Brian learned from the situation. Brian learned that Jane needed feedback on what was going well, and Jane learned to ask for input on priorities before reallocating work.

Too many people think they first have to give good feedback in order to also give bad feedback. I wish I had a dollar for every time I heard someone say, *"Well, I've got to say something positive and fluff people up so they don't freak out when I give negative feedback."* This is utterly wrong. Leave the empathy sandwich—where you say something good, slip in bad news, and then cushion it with more good news—to customer service representatives.

At some point your coworkers will both exceed your expectations and disappoint you. They'll go out of their way to be helpful, teach you something you need to know, or compliment your work in front of your boss. They'll also miss deadlines, forget to keep you informed, and ignore protocol. Pick your battles—address the big missteps and perhaps overlook the small. But remember, if you want the things you appreciate to be repeated, make sure you acknowledge the good stuff.

Given that I've just stressed that you should give positive feedback, it may appear contradictory that the next several pages will provide explicit instructions on how to give negative feedback and won't mention how to deliver positive feedback. The "rules" of giving positive and negative feedback are the same. I'll focus on giving negative feedback because it's so much harder to give than positive feedback—not because negative feedback is more important.

KNOWING WHEN TO **SHUT UP**

Before we talk about how to give feedback, let's talk about what feedback is and what it isn't. There are two purposes for providing feedback: To either change behavior or maintain it. *There are no other reasons.*

Mark, one of my colleagues from a previous job, applied for a position in a different department. After weeks of interviewing, three candidates remained who were considered finalists. Mark was offered the job and was really excited. On the day he received the offer, Mark swung by the new department to thank the team for the job and say how flattered he was to have been their first choice.

Joe, a guy on the team, didn't like Mark and promptly let him know that he was not the team's first choice; in fact, he was their last choice. The two other candidates declined the position and Mark was the last option.

Was Joe giving feedback? No. He wasn't trying to change an aspect of Mark's behavior nor encourage him to continue a behavior. Telling Mark he was the team's last choice was a pure zinger. This is a no-no, yet we've all done it. We're annoyed about something but haven't said anything, and our frustration oozes out in the form of a potshot.

Instead of taking potshots when you're frustrated, I suggest a practice I call "check your motives at the door." Before you speak, ask yourself, *"Is my intention to change the person's behavior or encourage its repetition?"* If you're not speaking for either purpose, shut up. All you're going to do is damage the relationship and your reputation.

Feedback is one ingredient in the recipe. It's not the whole meal. It's not always appropriate, desired, or necessary to tell people what you think.

Give feedback when

- ▸ the person asked for your opinion;
- ▸ you asked for and were given permission to give input, and you have a specific example to share;

▸ the incident happened recently, preferably within a week;

▸ you are trying to help the person improve her performance or want to be sure she keeps doing something that is working.

Don't give feedback when

▸ you're annoyed and it's a chance to express your frustration;

▸ you don't like this person and this seems like a perfect time to tell her;

▸ she hasn't asked for feedback but clearly needs it;

▸ you don't have permission;

▸ it's a good chance to blast someone in front of others.

NOW THAT YOU KNOW WHEN TO SPEAK UP, WHAT ARE YOU GOING TO SAY?

You've asked your coworkers for permission to give feedback and have offered to give it to them. So what are you going to say if they ask? Most of us avoid giving feedback like we avoid going to the dentist. We know we should go every six months but often don't until we're writhing in pain and need a root canal. Giving feedback is similar.

We watch our coworkers do things that negatively impact their careers. We see the impending catastrophe and, for the most part, say nothing, thinking it's not our place to comment.

Here's a true-life example: I was at a client site talking to an employee who was describing the impending train wreck in her department. She described projects that were poorly planned and inadequately staffed. She was telling me exactly what would happen as a result.

"This is going to explode. We're going to miss deadlines. Clients will complain and the entire department will be in the office evenings and weekends, trying to get things out the door. It's totally predictable," she explained.

I asked if she had told this to Linda, the leader of the department. "No," she said.

"Why not?" I asked.

She shrugged her shoulders and said, "Why bother? She doesn't really want to know."

This happens all the time, in every company, everywhere. It's easier to say nothing than risk telling the truth.

We've talked about how to ask people for permission to both give and receive feedback. You must have permission. If you don't, input will be very difficult to give and even more difficult for the recipient to hear.

Unsolicited feedback reminds us of a nagging mom. We know she wants what's best for us, but her advice can be really annoying. Without asking for and gaining permission to speak up, you haven't earned the right to say anything, so keep your opinions to yourself.

Even when you have permission to give feedback within a trusting relationship, recipients will get defensive. If they don't, be worried. If you give someone negative feedback and he doesn't get even a wee bit defensive, he is dead, doesn't care, or is hearing impaired.

A manager I used to coach had an employee with significant performance issues. Jeff was struggling with what to tell his direct report and how. So we drafted the conversation, honing the message until it was just right. After he spoke to the employee, Jeff called to tell me how it went.

"I said everything we practiced, and she got really defensive. Isn't it her job to accept my feedback graciously? I see her defensiveness as yet another performance issue."

I wanted to say, "*And you're an idiot.*" But I didn't. Jeff simply forgot that people are human, and it's natural to get defensive.

HUMAN BEINGS ARE WIRED
TO **DEFEND THEMSELVES**

Remember how when you were little, your parents taught you to look both ways before you crossed the street? They did this so you wouldn't get run over by a Mack truck. Becoming defensive when receiving negative feedback serves the same purpose for adults. It helps keep us safe.

No one wants to be told he is doing a bad job. Despite how it may seem with some of your coworkers, people don't wake up on Monday mornings wondering, *"How can I mess things up today? Who can I annoy? What should I turn in late, riddled with errors?"*

On the contrary, most human beings have a need to be seen as good, if not perfect. When someone calls our performance into question, it's normal and natural to defend ourselves. It's so normal and so natural that it's automatic. We don't even see ourselves doing it.

Rather than dread feedback recipients' defensiveness, expect it. See it as validation that you're not working with an avatar.

Elisabeth Kübler-Ross discussed the S.A.R.A.H. model in her book, *On Death and Dying*. Kübler-Ross described the process—shock, anger, resistance, acceptance, and hope—that all human beings go through when they're confronted with the loss of a loved one.

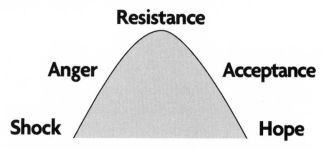

The S.A.R.A.H. model was later applied to people receiving negative feedback and going through a major change in the workplace. At first, we are shocked, then angry, and then resistant, before finally coming to a state of acceptance and hope.

Everybody goes through these stages at his or her own pace. Some people take days to reach a state of acceptance; others take weeks. But we all go through the stages. While the person providing the feedback can't and won't eliminate defensiveness on the part of the person who receives it, he can reduce the defensiveness and shorten the time it takes people to move through the stages. The next few pages will explain how to deliver feedback in a way that reduces recipients' defensiveness.

MOST FEEDBACK IS LIKE **CAP'N CRUNCH**

As the leader of learning and development in a previous position, I managed the organization's succession planning process and read hundreds of performance appraisals. Most of the appraisals could have belonged to anyone; they were so vague, they were interchangeable.

A typical appraisal read like this: "Rob is a great team player. He worked really hard this year and did good work. He added a lot of value to the organization."

That's very nice, but it's just not useful. Unfortunately, this is what most of the feedback we both give and receive is like. Kind of like Cap'n Crunch, the sweet, crunchy kids' breakfast cereal— all the flavor, but none of the nutrients.

Hearing that things are going fine or that we should just keep doing what we're doing is like eating Cap'n Crunch. It tastes good, but it's not useful. Feedback that is detailed and specific is more like the breakfast adults know they should eat, packed with nutrients that are essential to being strong and fit. Like healthy food, specific feedback feeds us, telling us what we need to do to achieve a desired result.

If you were on a diet and got on an electronic scale that lit up with the words "Not bad, keep up the good work," you'd return the scale because it didn't work. Useful feedback is specific. It describes what happened, the consequences of your actions, and an alternative way to do something in the future. It contains both attributes (adjectives, adverbs, and sometimes nouns) and behaviors (verbs that describe what the person did).

"Rob is a good team player" cites only attributes. It says nothing about the actions Rob took that made him a good team member. Thus he has no idea what to keep doing. If Rob repeats the behavior that made him a good team player it will be by chance, not because of anything he was told.

Useful feedback for Rob would describe the actions he took that made him a good team player. Then he would know what actions to continue doing. Instead, Rob received a feel-good appraisal that offered no guidance.

Here are several examples of attributes and behaviors:

Attributes (Cap'n Crunch)	Behaviors (Specific Feedback)
Team player	Offers to help others on the team even when it's not his job.
Hardworking	Does whatever needs to be done to get the job done. Is often seen in the office on weekends.
Difficult to work with	Questions every decision.
Good worker	Produces work that is accurate and complete.
Thorough	Submits work that covers all the details.
Aggressive	Raises his voice in meetings when he is frustrated.

RECEIVING EFFECTIVE FEEDBACK IS LIKE WATCHING A VIDEO

Good feedback is specific. It's like watching a video. The person providing the feedback replays what happened by describing the situation. This specific description allows the feedback recipient to remember and relive the experience. When recipients remember the specific situation and their actions, defensiveness goes down and receptivity goes up. People are less likely to argue with feedback when they can picture the situation and remember what they did or didn't do.

When a vivid description of what happened is provided, true feedback has been delivered. When this behavior-based description is missing and feedback is only attribute based, the input is not actually feedback. It's merely moving air around the room, with a little noise mixed in.

IF YOU CAN'T GIVE AN EXAMPLE,
YOU'RE NOT READY TO GIVE FEEDBACK

If you want to be sure people get really defensive, give vague feedback. Anytime feedback can be interpreted in more than one way, it's too vague.

Remember the example of Mark, the third choice for his new job? Mark had applied for the same job six months earlier and was rejected. The hiring committee thought he was arrogant and thus didn't want him on their team. Wanting to be helpful, the hiring manager told Mark when he didn't get the job initially that the team felt he was arrogant. It wasn't a surprise that Mark became extremely defensive.

Arrogant means different things to different people and can be demonstrated in many ways. Telling Mark he is arrogant is unhelpful, but telling him specific behaviors and actions that made him appear arrogant is quite helpful. Without knowing the specific behaviors that created that unfavorable impression, Mark was left with guesswork, which created paranoia and defensiveness.

When people get vague feedback, they become confused and start to ask around. They approach others and ask questions: *"I got feedback that I'm arrogant. What do you think that means? Do you think I'm arrogant?"*

Again, the purpose of feedback is to change behavior or reinforce it. The hiring manager didn't give Mark enough information for him to change his behavior. The manager should have either said nothing or asked the team what specific behaviors he could share with Mark.

The manager later discovered that Mark had a reputation for telling other people what to do, even those people who were "above" him in title and level. Mark also liked to be "in the know" about what was happening in the organization. Mark would gather data and tell his peers that big things were coming, but he was unable to reveal what those "big things" were. These behaviors were part of what made him appear arrogant. Those examples made for clear, specific, and thus useful feedback for the hiring manager to provide.

SUMMARY: *FEEDBACK IS THE DATA YOU NEED IN ORDER TO DIRECT YOUR CAREER AND BUSINESS RESULTS.*

Think of feedback as food. Specific feedback is the nutrition you need to make good career choices. Knowing how you're being perceived allows you to choose to keep doing what you're doing or to choose to do something different. And choice is a type of power, and power gives you more control of your outcomes.

In the next few chapters we'll talk about how to both give and get more useful feedback. Both strategies will enable you to drive your career and business relationships.

CHAPTER 10

THE FEEDBACK **FORMULA**

I suspect many of you picked up this book just to get the formula to tell people around you how annoying they are. Well, here it is. You've made it through most of the book, so you've earned it.

Below are eight steps that will enable you to say anything—no matter how difficult—in two minutes or less.

1. Introduce the conversation by explaining what you're going to talk about and why.

2. Empathize.

3. Describe the observed behavior.

4. Share the impact or result of the behavior.

5. Have some dialogue, and ask the recipient for his perception of the situation.

6. Make a suggestion or request for what you'd like the person to do next time.

7. Build an agreement on next steps (if any).

8. Say "Thank you."

Conversations following these eight steps enable recipients to remember the situation, see the impact of their actions, speak on their own behalf, and create, hopefully with your input, a plan for the future.

Below is more information about the purpose of following each of the eight feedback steps.

1. **INTRODUCE THE CONVERSATION** so feedback recipients know what to expect.

2. **EMPATHIZE** so both the feedback provider and the recipient feel as comfortable as possible.

3. **DESCRIBE THE OBSERVED BEHAVIOR** so the recipient can picture a specific, recent example of what you're referring to. The more specific you are, the less defensive he will be, and the more likely he'll be to hear you and take corrective action.

4. **SHARING THE IMPACT OR RESULT** describes the consequences of the behavior. It's what happened as a result of the person's actions.

5. **HAVING SOME DIALOGUE** gives both people a chance to speak and ensures that the conversation is not one-sided. Many feedback conversations are not conversations at all; they're monologues. One person talks and the other person pretends to listen, while thinking what an idiot you are. Good feedback conversations are dialogues during which the recipient can ask questions, share his point of view, and explore next steps.

6. **MAKE A SUGGESTION OR REQUEST** so the recipient has another way to approach the situation or task in the future. Most feedback conversations tell the person what he did wrong and the impact of the behavior; only rarely do they offer an alternative. Give people the benefit of the doubt. If people knew a better way to do something, they would do it another way.

7. **BUILDING AN AGREEMENT ON NEXT STEPS** ensures there is a plan for what the person will do going forward.

Too many feedback conversations do not result in behavior change. Agreeing on next steps creates accountability.

8. **SAY "THANK YOU"** to create closure and to express appreciation for the recipient's willingness to have a difficult conversation.

If you're giving more than one piece of feedback during a conversation, address each issue individually. For example, if you need to tell someone that she needs to arrive on time and also check her work for errors, first go through the eight steps in the formula to address lateness. When you've discussed an agreement of next steps about being on time, go back to step one and address the errors. But talk about one issue at a time so the person clearly understands what she's supposed to do.

REMOVE THE EMOTION AND DEAL WITH THE FACTS; HOW YOU FEEL MAKES NO DIFFERENCE

The eight-step Feedback Formula is short, simple, and straightforward. But something is deliberately missing. The Formula focuses on the facts—not on how you feel about the person or situation.

It may be the tenth time you've had the same conversation without seeing any behavior change, and you are rightfully exasperated. But saying so won't make a difference. It will just make the other person feel bad. While that might sound appealing in the moment, it won't help change the other person's behavior.

Feedback with a zinger reminds me of my eighth-grade Spanish teacher, Señora Wells, a short, stout woman who was renowned throughout the school for her daily footwear—rhinestone slippers. After I screwed up the masculine and feminine endings of every word on yet another test, she stood with one hand on her hip, rolled her eyes, and sighed, "I simply cannot explain this to you again."

That statement was all about her frustration and not at all about my ineptitude at grasping a romance language. Telling me

"I don't think you're cut out to speak Spanish" would have been much more useful and much less hurtful.

Too often feedback conversations contain the following phrases:

"I'm so disappointed in you."

"I can't believe we're having this conversation again."

"I'm so frustrated."

How you as the feedback giver feels is not part of the Feedback Formula because the conversation is not about you. It's about the other person and the impact of her behavior.

Rather than saying, *"I'm so disappointed in you,"* how about saying, *"Your (specific) behavior is reflecting negatively on the department. If it continues, I will have to put you in a less visible position on the team."*

Rather than saying, *"I can't believe we're having this conversation again,"* how about saying, *"We've talked about this several times and there has been no change. Megan has offered to mentor you, and I think it's a good idea. Perhaps her feedback will be clearer."*

Rather than saying, *"I'm so frustrated,"* how about saying, *"We've talked about this several times and I've not seen measured improvement. To be honest, I'm not sure what to do next. What suggestions do you have?"*

WHEN DO YOU **CUT BAIT?**

Addressing the same behavior multiple times begs the question: At what point do you stop giving feedback and either end relationships or work around people?

There's a point at which you (a) give up and fire an employee, (b) rotate him to a job where he can be more successful, or (c) get him moved off a project or account and then work with the people who remain. That's an unfortunate reality.

But no matter the outcome, you can do the right thing by giving specific feedback in a timely way. If after a reasonable number of attempts you don't see sufficient change, work with the people who will work with you.

If you've given the same feedback several times without seeing a change in the other person's behavior, it's easy to become discouraged. Instead of giving up, I'd ask myself what consequences the person is facing for not changing her behavior. If the same feedback has been given repeatedly with little or no evidence of behavior change, I'd say the consequences as described have been minimal or simply not enough to motivate the person to change.

As simple as it sounds, people change their behavior for two reasons—positive and negative consequences. If I could eat cookies, ice cream, chocolate icing, and nothing else and not be the size of a house, I'd do it. But I can't, so I don't. It's as simple as that.

IF YOU'RE REALLY WORRIED ABOUT THEIR FEELINGS, **YOU'LL BE DIRECT**

If you follow the Feedback Formula, your conversations will be short and direct. But most of us don't use this approach. Instead, we uncomfortably dance around an issue, and that dancing creates longer and more uncomfortable conversations than are necessary.

When I teach feedback skills in organizations, I always have participants practice with one of the most difficult situations possible—telling someone he or she smells. Who wants to tell anyone that? But if you work with or manage people long enough, you will eventually be in this situation.

I give class participants the Formula and let them go at it. This is what they usually say: *"Well, uh, John, I need to talk with you about something, mmm . . . a little awkward. It, uh, well, mmm. It has come to my attention, well actually, others in the office have talked about it. Well, I've heard that you have an, um, well, an odor."*

THE WORDS **"I'VE NOTICED"** ARE YOUR FRIEND

Time and again I watch people talk in circles, using many more words than necessary and saying very little. During training sessions, these tongue-stumbling participants explain that they are "just trying to be nice." Dancing around an issue and taking longer than necessary to deliver a difficult message isn't nice. Nice is direct—using the fewest words possible to convey a clear and specific message. When you are direct, you do the person a favor. You give him nutrients, not Cap'n Crunch; you give the person the power to make a different choice, if he or she chooses to do that.

Many people tend to pin the source of the negative feedback on colleagues; this indirect approach creates suspicion and paranoia. Just share what you've observed and the recipient will get the message. There's no need to implicate other people in the organization. Doing so only damages relationships and breaks trust.

If you haven't observed the behavior directly and instead someone told you about it, attempt to witness what the person is doing or not doing yourself. Feedback that begins with "I've noticed" has a lot more power and is easier to hear than "It's come to my attention" or "A few members of the team are concerned about . . . "

When you start a conversation with someone else's observations, the other person's defensive reaction goes up and she can't hear what you're saying. All she can think about is being betrayed by someone who didn't have the guts to speak to her directly.

There are times when it's simply not possible to observe behavior directly, and you'll have to tell the person you heard the feedback from someone else. While this is never ideal, it's still better to share it—provided you've validated the feedback and it impacts the person significantly. The person needs the feedback and deserves to get it, regardless of the source.

When you're delivering feedback on behalf of another person, I suggest encouraging the recipient to take the feedback for what it is—food in the form of data. Encourage her to see the benefit of getting the information and to focus on what she wants to do differently, rather than on finding out who said what. And know that even when you suggest she not do this, the first thing most people will do when leaving your office is go straight to the source and ask (demand) to know why he didn't talk with her directly. But even this is better than someone being in the dark about what she does that's ineffective. I'll take worry and even temporary anger over ignorance any day.

Okay, back to body-odor guy. Here's how the conversation could sound, using the eight-step Feedback Formula:

STEP ONE: Introduce the conversation.

"John, I need to talk with you."

STEP TWO: Empathize.

"This is a little awkward, and it may be uncomfortable. I want you to know that while I wish I didn't have to tell you this, I'm doing it because I care about you and I want you to be successful."

Just because you're direct doesn't mean you're not empathetic. But remember, these are my words. You'll need to find your own words that you feel comfortable using to deliver such a difficult message.

STEP THREE: Describe the observed behavior.

"John, I've noticed that you have an odor."

STEP FOUR: Share the impact or result of the behavior.

"I know this is a very awkward subject (more empathy). We work in a small space. I don't want others to avoid working with you or say negative things about you. And as awkward as this is, I would rather you hear this from me than from someone else. Sometimes health conditions can cause certain odors, as can eating certain foods."

STEP FIVE: Have some dialogue. Ask the recipient for his perception of the situation.

"What are your thoughts?"

Give John time to say whatever he wishes to say.

STEP SIX: Make a suggestion or request for what to do next time.

> *"Again, I'm really sorry to have to tell you this. Please make sure you shower every day before coming to work and wash your clothes regularly. And please tell me if there's something else you'd like me to know."*

Because of the awkwardness of this subject, skip STEP SEVEN, and go to STEP EIGHT.

> *"Thank you for being willing to have this conversation with me."*

> **Watch a video of the author demonstrating this conversation at:**
> www.leadershipandsalestraining.com/sayanything

YOU CAN SAY **MORE** THAN YOU THINK YOU CAN

You might be gasping, thinking there is no way you could ever tell someone he smells. It's definitely an awkward conversation, one I hope you never have to have. I used one of the most difficult things you will ever have to say to demonstrate that even the most awkward feedback can be delivered empathetically and quickly.

The short and concise body-odor conversation is a lot less uncomfortable for the recipient than the drawn-out, evasive first version. Just think, would you rather listen to someone tell you that you smell for two minutes or for twenty?

You may also think, *"I shouldn't have to tell someone to take a shower and wash their clothes."* That's true, you shouldn't. But if you're working with someone who doesn't do these things, clearly someone needs to tell him. Remember, other people are not you and don't do things the way you do, even when those things appear to be no-brainer basics.

Lastly, you may think that telling someone to shower and wash his clothes is insulting and demeaning. It's true: No matter how you spin it, there's nothing nice about this message. But which is worse, having your coworkers ask for different desks and be unwilling to work with you, or having someone who has your best interests at heart tell you privately to clean it up—quite literally? When you tell people the truth, you do them a favor.

Here's another example: A few years ago I had a coworker who was a lingerer. Lisa would hover outside my office until she saw an opportunity to interrupt. She then walked in uninvited and started talking. I was still mid-thought about whatever I'd been working on and wasn't ready to listen. After a few sentences, I would interrupt Lisa, saying, "I'm sorry. I don't know what you're talking about. Will you please start over?"

Embarrassing as it sounds, this went on for more than a year. I wanted to be seen as accessible and open, yet this "lingering" method of interrupting was driving me crazy. And it was a waste of time for both of us. After many months of frustration, I decided to use the eight-step Formula.

STEP ONE: Introduce the conversation.

"Lisa, I want to talk about something I've noticed."

STEP TWO: Empathize.

"I probably should have said something a long time ago. I'm sorry I didn't."

STEP THREE: Describe the observed behavior.

"I've noticed that when you want to talk to me you stand at my door, waiting for a good time to interrupt. When you come into my office, you're often in the middle of a thought or problem that you've probably been thinking about for a while."

STEPS FOUR and SIX: Share the impact or result of the behavior and make a suggestion or request for what to do next time.

"Because I'm in the middle of something completely different, it takes me a few seconds to catch up. By the time I have, I've missed key points about your question and I have to ask you to start over. This isn't a good use of either of our time.

"Here is my request: When I'm in my office working and you need something, knock and ask if it's a good time. If it is, I'll say yes. Give me a few seconds to finish whatever I'm working on, so I'm focused on you when we start talking. I'll tell you when I'm ready. Then start at the beginning, giving me a little background, so I have some context. And if it isn't a good time for me, I'll tell you that and come find you as soon as I can."

STEP FIVE: Have some dialogue. Allow the recipient to say whatever she needs to say.

"What do you think?"

STEP SEVEN: Agree on next steps.

"Okay, so next time you want to talk with me, you're going to tap on the door and ask if it's a good time to talk. If it's not, I'll tell you that and come find you as soon as I can. If it is a good time, you're going to give me a second to finish whatever I'm working on and give me some background about the issue at hand. Does that work for you?"

We have just managed "the lingerer"—a challenge you probably have, unless you work from home or in a closet.

You may have noticed that I changed the order of the Feedback Formula during this conversation. It's not the order of the conversation that's important. It's that you provide specific feedback, offer alternative actions, and have some dialogue before the conversation ends.

SUMMARY: *GOOD FEEDBACK IS SPECIFIC, SUCCINCT, AND DIRECT.*

Provided you have a trusting relationship with someone and have secured permission to give feedback, there is very little you can't say in two minutes or less. The shorter and more direct the message, the easier it is to hear and act upon. Follow the eight-step Feedback Formula. Be empathetic and direct. Cite specific examples. Give the other person a chance to talk. Come to agreement about next steps. Remember, you do people a favor by being honest with them. People may not like what you have to say, but they will invariably thank you for being candid.

CHAPTER 11

TIPS FOR GIVING
USEFUL FEEDBACK

Feedback conversations can strengthen your relationships and build trust. I know that sounds funny. Telling someone she did something that bugged you builds rapport? Yes, it does. When you are willing to have a difficult conversation, you demonstrate that you care about the person and the relationship. If you didn't care, you'd say nothing, tell other people, cut the person off, or work around her.

EMAIL IS FOR WIMPS AND
VOICEMAIL ISN'T MUCH BETTER

When you have something difficult to say, sending an email or leaving a voicemail is easier than having a live conversation. You can hone what you want to say until your message is just right. You can manage your emotions and you don't have to deal with the other person's reaction.

But you can't manage your tone in an email, see the other person's response, or ensure she hears your message as you intended it.

A string of emails or voicemails does not make a conversation. And despite the prevalence of online dating and the pleasure we take in maintaining friendships through Facebook, email alone does not build a relationship. Try telling your friends you're dating or are married to someone you've never met in person. They'll have you committed, and it won't be to the Hilton.

Giving feedback via email and voicemail is for wimps. Suck it up. Ask permission to give feedback. Have a live conversation. Neither of you will die. And the more often you have these conversations, the easier they become. The first few conversations will be stressful. Your stomach will probably be in your mouth. You'll be anxious and so will they. But it will get easier.

It's a little like dating. The first few times you go out with someone, you probably spend a long time getting ready. By the fifth date you might warn your date not to expect great things because you're coming from the gym. What's the difference between the first and the fifth date? It's your degree of comfort. Just as you become comfortable with new people, you'll become more comfortable giving negative feedback. It will never be easy, but it will become easier.

I'm often asked how to give feedback to employees who work in a different location. Here's the answer: Call them. There's almost nothing you can't say over the phone, beyond telling someone they've been laid off or fired. You can have performance discussions, tell her she's getting a new boss, rotate projects, etc.

You don't need to be sitting in front of someone to have a meaningful conversation. But if you can't get over feeling that the phone is impersonal, get on Skype and video chat. That will require employees who telecommute to take a shower and get dressed for work, but it will be good for them to get out of their jammies once in a while.

THE NEW **NICE**

I was on the phone with a friend a few weeks ago when he informed me that he was nice—and I wasn't. He went on to say,

"You're direct. You tell people what you're thinking. If someone does something that frustrates you, you're going to tell them. I won't. So I'm nice and you're not."

I was flabbergasted.

Let me get this straight. It's nice to watch people damage their careers and say nothing? And it's not nice to tell people the things they do that kill their reputation, which gives them a chance to do something about those missteps? That makes no sense to me.

I'll have lunch with this same friend and lettuce will be stuck between my teeth, but he won't say anything. Or after visiting the restroom I'll have toilet paper stuck to the bottom of my shoe, and he won't say anything. How is it nice to let someone return to work and sit in a meeting with lettuce in her teeth and toilet paper on her shoe? That's not nice. It's wimpy and doesn't make for good friend or coworker material.

The conversation with my "nice" friend made me a think of one of my new vendors. If I email him a request and he doesn't know what to say or doesn't want to do what I'm asking, he just doesn't get back to me. That's brilliant: Just ignore me. That's definitely not the way to handle a client's needs. He probably thinks I'll eventually forget the request and he'll be off the hook. Instead, I've decided he's a big wimp whom I don't respect. I'm starting to see a theme.

It seems that one definition of *nice* is "to disempower your friends and colleagues by saying nothing when they've done something stupid or are about to walk off a cliff. Instead of saving them from career suicide, pretend you haven't seen or heard anything. Because to speak up and actually be helpful is rude, otherwise known as not "nice."

I'm on a crusade to redefine nice. How about this definition instead:

Nice is asking permission to be honest with people when they do something that is potentially career limiting. It's telling the truth, as you see it, once you've been granted permission. It's demonstrating that you have someone's back and you would rather he hear bad news from you, even if it's uncomfortable, rather than from someone who can fire him or prevent him from being promoted.

Though many may prefer my friend's definition of nice—to say nothing when others commit career-limiting moves—I'll continue to be "direct" any day, and I hope you will, too.

REAL RELATIONSHIPS REQUIRE **COURAGE**

I can't count the number of times I've been told, "I can't tell him that; it will hurt his feelings." Or, "I didn't say anything because I was trying to be nice."

Not getting promoted and not knowing why hurts more than being told that your work is often late and contains errors, and that you're considered unreliable. Being gossiped about throughout the office hurts more than being told that it's disruptive when you raise your voice in meetings, and that this has earned you the reputation of being someone who's difficult to work with.

Useful feedback involves all the guidelines we're discussing here. It requires two valuable human traits: courage and the desire to make a difference for someone.

It takes guts to tell someone she is not meeting expectations, that she has body odor, or that she runs ineffective meetings. Laying the groundwork for feedback discussions by asking permission will help a lot, but these conversations are still hard. No one wants to hear those things, and as a result, no one wants to say them. But I assure you, people would rather know and thus be in a position to manage the situation than unknowingly suffer negative consequences because of their behavior.

In addition to giving clear and specific feedback focused on the facts (not on how you feel), there are a number of things you can do to help people absorb what you have to say while reducing their defensiveness. One is to give feedback shortly after an event occurs, while it's still fresh in the person's mind.

The purpose of feedback is to shift or reinforce behavior. When you provide someone with feedback, it helps if the person can clearly remember the situation you're talking about. If you wait to address an issue that happened several weeks or months ago, people may not remember the situation and you will appear to be someone who holds a grudge.

MANAGE, RESOLVE, AND **MOVE ON**

Don't be a person who never lets anything go, waiting for someone to repeat a behavior and then pouncing on him when he does. Deal with what comes up soon after it happens. Say whatever you need to say, then move on and let the other person do so as well.

Every time I conduct a training session on providing limited amounts of feedback—just one or two areas for improvement at a time—someone in the audience gasps audibly. A hand goes up, followed by this question. "There are so many things I need to address. How can I just choose one or two?" My response: "How long have these things that you want to address been going on?" And then there's always a long pause.

If you've waited several weeks or more to address an issue, consider it a missed opportunity. If the behavior is a problem, wait for it to happen again; when it does, address it immediately. If the behavior isn't repeated, you don't need to address it.

PRACTICE THE 24-HOUR GUIDELINE AND THE ONE-WEEK RULE

Give feedback within a week of an incident. If you're upset or the other person is upset, wait twenty-four hours or until both of you are calm and can have a rational conversation. Just don't wait three or four weeks, when whatever happened will have become a distant memory.

Give feedback as close to the event as possible, provided the following conditions exist:

▶ You're not upset and your emotions will not run the conversation.

▶ The feedback recipient is not upset and can hear what you have to say.

▶ You have sufficient time to have a conversation—that is, neither of you is running to a meeting or leaving to catch a train in the next ten minutes.

▶ The recipient is not having a day during which everything has gone wrong: His kids are sick; his car had a flat tire on the way in to work; he had a fender bender during his lunch break, etc. You need the recipient to be able to focus on the conversation, not on the logistical nightmare that has become his day.

▶ Neither of you are going on vacation the next day. You want people to have a chance to think about what you said and come back to you with questions.

Be careful. There's a fine line between waiting to provide feedback until the timing is right and waiting because you're avoiding the conversation. The two can be confused, but they are distinctly different. Wait until you're calm but not so long that neither of you can accurately remember the details of what occurred. The intention of providing feedback is to change or reinforce behavior. People can't change behavior they don't remember.

FEEDBACK AND THE LAW OF DIMINISHING RETURNS

Let's say it's January 1 and you're creating New Year's resolutions or personal goals. You're feeling ambitious. Your goals may look something like this: Exercise five times a week; get out of debt; quit smoking; pursue hobbies; volunteer once a week; improve the landscaping around the house; and make 30 percent more money.

Rather than annual goals, this list should be called "How I set myself up to fail in one sitting."

People can't focus on ten things at a time. It's impossible. Watch a good athletic coach. He gives one instruction at a time, allowing students to practice that one technique until they've got it down and are ready to add more. Treat the people you work with the same way.

- Give small amounts of feedback—no more than three things to work on at one time, preferably one or two.
- Acknowledge progress if you see behavior changes.
- Address those things that still haven't changed.

My last recommendation, which helps to reduce defensiveness and ensure people can hear what you have to say, is to give feedback privately. If you want to guarantee that someone will get defensive, give her feedback in front of other people or in a cubicle where it's almost certain others can hear the conversation. The recipient will be so embarrassed or worried that others are listening that she won't hear a thing you're saying and will immediately distrust you. Giving negative feedback in front of others has damaged many relationships, often permanently. Make friends with your company's conference rooms and use them for feedback conversations. And if conference rooms and empty offices are scarce, find a nearby coffee shop that the rest of your office doesn't frequent.

GOOD FEEDBACK CONVERSATIONS ARE **PLANNED**

Feedback conversations are stressful. To ensure you say everything you want to say, plan your conversations.

About ten years ago, I had a manager who was often volatile, unpredictable, and irrational. To describe Kathryn as difficult to work with was an understatement. Talking with her was beyond stressful. I would get so nervous during our meetings that I'd forget to discuss half the things I wanted to say. It was a little like going to a doctor who is so rushed that as you walk out of his office you realize you didn't ask the questions that led you to his office in the first place. So I started preparing for our meetings.

Before each meeting I made a bulleted list of everything I wanted to talk about and practiced particularly difficult conversations out loud. If you've done any public speaking, you know that saying something in your head is very different from saying it aloud. When Kathryn became emotional and I became flustered, I would look at my list, check off the last thing we talked about, and move to the next item. Having notes of what I wanted to say kept me calm and ensured that I got what I needed from our very stressful meetings.

What follows is a series of questions for you to consider writing down the answers to as you plan for difficult feedback conversations.

- ▸ **What's working?**
- ▸ **What's not working?**
- ▸ **What's most important for this person to know?**
- ▸ **What would you like this person to do differently?**
- ▸ **What are your requests?**
- ▸ **What do you want to say but know you probably won't?**
- ▸ **What will you say first?**

SAYING IT "ALL WRONG" IS BETTER THAN SAYING NOTHING AT ALL!

Most important, have courage. Even if you forget every best practice, guideline, and suggestion here, and you do it "all wrong," saying something is better than saying nothing at all. Telling someone the truth gives her power she didn't have before.

If you say the wrong thing or your message comes out stronger than you would like, apologize. If you hurt someone's feelings, say you're sorry. She'll recover from a tough message faster than from applying for the same job three times, not getting it, and not knowing why. The people you work with are tougher than you think, and so are you.

SUMMARY: *IF YOU CARE ABOUT THE PEOPLE YOU WORK WITH, BE HONEST WITH THEM.*

It's easier to say nothing about frustrating behavior than to address it. But saying nothing will not improve the situation or your working relationship. Despite how they might respond, the people you work with really do want to know the things they do that both improve and damage their credibility. When you're willing to tell people the truth, you do them a favor.

Find your courage and say what you need to say, in person, not via email or voicemail. Ask permission to give feedback and make sure it's a good time for the recipient. Take the time to plan the conversation. Be specific and timely, and provide examples. Address one or two things at a time, not six or seven. Despite the resistance you might receive, you'll earn your coworker's loyalty and trust.

CHAPTER 12

WHAT THEY SAY WHEN
YOU'RE NOT THERE

A re you wondering how to find out what people are saying about you when you're not there? The answer is simple—ask! Here are some techniques to learn about your
reputation.

People have a tendency to talk about us, not to us. This is an
unfortunate reality that, unless you live in a cave, you are already
aware of.

Fifteen years ago I learned a very painful lesson that forever
altered how I approach my career. I left a job I loved and took a
technical training job in an industry I knew nothing about. The
company put me in its ten-week, new-hire training program. When
the class ended, I was scheduled to teach the next one.

I was working at a satellite office. The four trainers teaching
the ten-week program came from the company headquarters,
about 1,000 miles away. My new colleagues had been traveling to
the satellite office to teach this program for the past five years and
were tired of living at the Marriott. The sooner I got up to speed,
the sooner they could go home to their families.

We were all about the same age, went to happy hour after work,
and quickly became friends. Wanting to succeed, I told my new
friends and coworkers that I wanted their feedback and asked them

to tell me if I did or said anything that got in the way of my success. They agreed they would do that. Sounds good so far, doesn't it?

Unfortunately, the material we discussed in training was extremely technical and completely foreign to me. I had no idea what we were talking about most of the time. Not wanting to appear clueless, I said absolutely nothing about my confusion. (Smart, right?) I knew that if I asked stupid questions, my fellow trainees would tell the incoming class that they had gotten the new trainer who didn't know anything. So I sat through each day of training not saying a word, hoping I wouldn't be found out.

Six weeks into the program my boss called me into her office. She said, "Shari, things are not going well for you here." (I knew that. But I'd been very quiet about it. I wondered how she knew.)

She continued, "I've gotten some feedback from your colleagues from the home office. They told me that you haven't asked any questions in training, and as a result they think you're arrogant and overly confident. They don't think you're taking this job seriously. I want you to go home and think about whether or not you want to work here, and come back tomorrow with a decision."

These were the same people whom I'd asked for feedback, the same "friends" I'd been hanging out with after work. And they went to my boss rather than coming to me. It was in that moment that I got that very hard and painful lesson—people talk about us, not to us.

That experience changed my life. I was angry, hurt, and confused. I wondered, *"Did I really come off as overly confident? Did the trainers honestly think I was arrogant?"* I didn't know how to reconcile the feedback, so I reached out to other people. I called my parents, two of my closest friends, and a few coworkers from my last job. I didn't call people who didn't like me or who had an ax to grind. I called people who I knew cared about me and who I thought would be honest with me. I told them I'd gotten some difficult feedback at work that I was trying to reconcile and asked if I could take them to lunch and ask a few questions. I promised that whatever they said, I would say thank you. And I promised to buy. (You must pay; this is very important!)

I wound up taking six people to lunch and asked each person the following questions:

1. What is the first impression I create?

2. What was I like to work with, or what do you think I would be like to work with?

3. If my coworkers were asked to talk about me when I wasn't there, what would they say?

4. How have I exceeded your expectations?

5. How have I disappointed you?

You won't be surprised to hear that I got some positive feedback and some negative feedback. But regardless of what my friends, family, and coworkers said, I said, "Thank you," even when I really wanted to argue or defend myself.

Those conversations weren't easy, but they were incredibly valuable. The most important thing I learned was that I didn't always know how I came across to other people.

DO YOU KNOW THE **IMPRESSION** YOU CREATE WITH OTHER PEOPLE?

Everything we do forms an impression: what we wear; the time we arrive at work; who we're friendly with in the office; the condition of our desk, etc. It's these little, seemingly insignificant things that can stifle our careers. If you wear clothing to work that is inappropriate for your office environment (stiletto heels that should only be worn when you're out for the evening or khakis that have never seen an iron), very few people will tell you. But they'll make a mental note that you may not be the best person to support key customers. Or perhaps they'll think you're not the most appropriate person to represent your boss at meetings when he's out of town.

I hired a new employee shortly before leaving a previous job. She was young and smart but, I came to learn, not politically savvy. Invariably when I walked through our lobby, Kate was standing at the receptionist's desk chatting. Not only did it look like she was squandering her and another employee's time, but she was leaning over the receptionist's desk, with her butt stuck out for the entire office to see. This was not the image we wanted portrayed in the lobby and hopefully not the image Kate wanted to portray of herself.

I also noticed that Kate typically had lunch with the assistant to the VP of sales, a person who was known throughout the office as lazy and unreliable. As a new employee, Kate's actions were creating others' impressions of her.

This will sound political, and it is. Kate, like all of us, was evaluated by the people she was seen with at work. People associate us with the people we hang out with. If you are seen with the hardworking, smart people, people will think you're hardworking and smart, until you prove them wrong. If you hang out with the people who gossip and are typically the source of office rumors, people will assume you don't keep confidences and are not trustworthy. Unfair and political as it may be, it's true.

Here's another example: A manager at a firm where I consult called me for advice. She heard that a staff member was unhappy and looking for another job. The manager wanted to know what she should do. The staff member was one of the firm's more talented employees, and losing him would be a big loss. She wanted to know if she should tell the director of the department that he was unhappy. I asked how she knew the staff member was looking. She told me, "Someone overheard him tell someone at happy hour. And that person told me." And this is how it goes.

A SECRET IS ONLY A SECRET
WHEN THE PERSON YOU TOLD IS **DEAD**

People talk. Even eighteen years in to my corporate career I am amazed at how much people talk about others and at how many things that are told in confidence are widely known. The lesson: Be careful whom you talk to and where you talk. Always assume that everything you tell someone at work will be told to someone else, even when the person you told promised to keep your confidence.

Impressions are formed quickly, and they're hard to change. As a result, it's important to know what people think about you and what they say when you're not there. Knowing what people think and say about you gives you the power to control what you put in front of others and take charge of your career.

Here's the bad news: You can't control what people think, feel, or say. But there is also good news: You can control what you put in front of people. You can change what you do, what you wear, and what time you show up to work, and thereby change how you are perceived. That is very good news, indeed.

If you're going to ask your colleagues for feedback, you have to be willing to hear whatever they have to say. You have also promised that you will respond to any feedback with "Thank you." This might not always be the easiest thing to do, depending on what the feedback actually is.

YOU **WANT** NEGATIVE FEEDBACK

While we hope that some feedback will be good, we hope some of it will also be bad—which probably sounds a little crazy. Why would you want anyone to give you negative feedback? Because without balanced and candid feedback you'll sit in your current job year in and year out, wondering why your career isn't going anywhere. Eventually you'll become frustrated and leave your company, only to quickly become pigeonholed in your next job.

The keys to being successful in business are the same everywhere, not just at your current organization. If you don't master those keys to success, your career will stagnate, wherever you are.

We all know there are things about our work habits and communication skills that could be improved. We know it, and our boss and colleagues know it. When others feel comfortable telling us what's not working, it's a sign that we've developed an authentic relationship. That level of comfort is very powerful. Knowing how we impact other people also gives us valuable information about how to proceed.

How many times have you asked for feedback and been told that everything is fine and to keep doing what you're doing? And then six months later, you get blasted in a performance review. "You're doing a great job" is nice to hear, but it isn't helpful.

Several years ago I worked for a woman whose favorite phrase was "Feedback is a gift." While her positive spin on verbal butt-kicking was annoying, she was right. Very few people will be honest with you; when someone takes off the kid gloves and tells you like it is, it's a gift. It's the most valuable thing anyone can do for you.

If feedback is so important but so rarely given, how do you find out how you're truly seen in your workplace?

ASK PEOPLE YOU TRUST FOR FEEDBACK

Find a few key people who care about your working relationship and who are direct. Don't seek feedback from the person in your office who hates you, covets your job, or has an ax to grind. Being direct is a risk; someone who cares about you might just take that risk.

The conversation could go something like this:

> *"We've been working together for a really long time. We see a lot of each other's work, and I realized that we never talk about it. I think it would be really helpful if we give each other feedback about what's*

working, and what we might do differently. What do you think? Is that something you'd like to do?"

"I've been working really hard strengthening my meeting facilitation skills. Would you be willing to watch me run a meeting and give me some feedback? I'd really appreciate your insights. In fact, I'd really like more feedback in general. If you'd be willing to bring things to my attention that get in the way of my success, I'd really appreciate it. I promise to be receptive and say thank you. Would you be comfortable doing that?"

Use the language that feels comfortable to you. Just don't be afraid to ask.

The people you work with are in a unique position to help you advance your career. They see you in action every day. They see you do things that make you look good and things that damage your reputation. But without an invitation, they're not likely to tell you. So open the door and give permission to give feedback. It's never too late.

You can also ask people from previous jobs and your friends and family for feedback. You may be surprised at how accurately close friends and family members can tell you what you do at work that is off-putting and getting in your way. You are who you are. You don't become a different person when you walk through your office doors. If you're late to work, you're probably also late to meet your family and friends. If you wear clothing that isn't flattering, you wear that clothing out to dinner, too. If you talk too much or too loud, or you don't keep confidences, your closest friends know that. Don't underestimate how much the people you have breakfast with can tell you about how you engage at work.

PEOPLE ARE WIRED TO **DEFEND THEMSELVES**

Negative information isn't easy to absorb. It often looms larger in our minds than perhaps it should. If your boss tells you five good things about your performance and one bad thing, what do you think about for the rest of the day? If you're like most people, you forget about the good stuff and focus on the bad.

Negative feedback always overshadows positive feedback. No one wants to be told she's wrong or that she disappointed someone. As a result, when human beings receive negative feedback, we overreact. And often we attempt to protect ourselves by becoming defensive. It's an automatic, hardwired response. There's nothing we can do about it. So just expect yourself to become defensive. Recognize it when you see it and manage your response, making it more likely you'll receive more feedback in the future.

When a few courageous souls tell you the truth, make it easy for them. Make the experience go down like candy, so they'll want to do it again. Anticipate becoming defensive and respond in a way that is counter to what the person you're talking to is expecting. People learn through experience. Become defensive and you'll get less feedback.

THE RIGHT ANSWER IS ALWAYS **"THANK YOU"**

The right answer to any type of feedback is "Thank you." Saying "Thank you" doesn't mean that the other person is right or that you agree. It means you heard the feedback and appreciate the risk that person took in telling you.

When receiving feedback, ask questions for more information and for clarification. Ask for examples if the feedback isn't specific. Regardless of how hard the feedback is to hear, don't defend yourself. Instead, ask permission to follow up later after you've had a chance to think about and digest the feedback.

Once you know what people are thinking and saying about you or your department, then leverage the positive things and begin to work on improving the not-so-positive things. Start small, with one thing at a time.

As human beings, we're most successful when we work on just one or two things at a time. So pick one behavior to leverage and one to improve. You can add additional behaviors to leverage and work on in ninety days or in six months. But for the moment, focus on the one or two things the person said that are most important to your success.

Consider telling your boss you've gotten some feedback and you'd really appreciate her input. You're probably going to catch her off guard. And you already know that most people aren't comfortable giving feedback. To set both of you up for success, consider starting the conversation like this:

> *"I got some feedback on _____. I respect your judgment and would like to hear your impressions. Would you be willing to watch for this behavior over the next two weeks? Then perhaps we can set a time to discuss your observations. Would that be okay?"*

By initiating this conversation, you've accomplished several things most people never even attempt.

Here is another example:

> *"Would you be willing to give me some feedback on how I run project kick-off meetings? I got some feedback on my last project that team members weren't 100 percent clear on their roles. Would you be willing to watch me lead a kick-off meeting and tell me what you think? I'm specifically looking for input on how I set expectations with the team. I want to be sure I lay out each team member's role and responsibilities for the next project. My next kick-off meeting is Wednesday at 2:00 p.m. If you can swing by or call in, that would be great. And if it's okay with you, I'll put a meeting on your calendar next week to discuss your observations."*

There are a few reasons to ask your supervisor for feedback on a specific piece of work or activity and then setting a future time to discuss the feedback. It's your boss's job to be knowledgeable about the things you're working on and to provide you with regular feedback. Making a blanket statement such as "I want more feedback" implies your boss isn't doing her job. Asking for specific feedback is much more subtle. Unless she follows you around all day, there is no way for her to be aware of your performance in all areas. (And unless you like being micromanaged, that's a good thing.)

By using this information-gathering strategy you've given some control to your boss and allowed her to save face, rather than putting her on the spot. It's embarrassing for a supervisor to be asked a question about your performance that she can't answer. By setting a specific time to discuss her feedback, you don't catch her off guard by asking for input on something she probably isn't thinking about and hasn't recently observed. Finally, you demonstrate that you are introspective, respect your boss's opinion, are open to her feedback, and are serious about your professional development. As a result, you'll get more thorough and thoughtful feedback.

> **Watch a video of the author demonstrating how to ask for feedback at:**
> www.leadershipandsalestraining.com/sayanything

GETTING MORE FEEDBACK **CHEAT SHEET**

Follow these steps and you will get more timely, specific, and candid feedback, making it easier to manage your business relationships and results. Don't assume things are going well or poorly. Ask for more information and graciously take whatever feedback you get.

1. Ask for feedback.

2. Promise you'll say "Thank you," regardless of what the person says.

3. Don't get defensive, even if you think she's wrong, because:

- ▸ The feedback is true for her.
- ▸ All you can deal with is the other person's experience.
- ▸ Your opinion of what happened makes no difference.

Next, tell the following five specifics to whomever you want feedback from:

1. I've been working on _____.

2. I'd really like your feedback.

3. I'd specifically like feedback on _____ and _____.

4. Here are the opportunities in the next two weeks to see me do this. (Or, please review this piece of work.)

5. Can we schedule a meeting to discuss?

Asking for feedback in this way puts the other person at ease and makes it more likely that you will get what you need. It also demonstrates that you're serious about your performance and that you value the other person's input.

TIPS FOR RESPONDING TO FEEDBACK

▸ Know that you will get defensive.

▸ Saying, "I don't mean to be defensive, but what I intended was . . ." is defensive.

▸ Just because you don't turn red, raise your voice, or vehemently disagree doesn't mean you're not being defensive.

▸ Almost anything you say to explain will sound defensive.

▸ Say "Thank you."

▸ Leave the conversation.

▸ Think about what the person said.

▸ Ask others for their input.

▸ When you're not upset, return to the person with questions, if necessary.

The less defensive you become, the more feedback you'll receive. Learning to handle all types of feedback is a necessary skill. If you're truly serious about moving ahead in your career, you will learn to do it.

Feedback is information, and information gives you the power to control your reputation and outcomes.

SUMMARY: KNOW YOUR BLIND SPOTS.

Successful professionals who work well with others are aware of the impressions they create and how they affect people. The problem is that very few people will tell you about the mistakes you make at work. It's easier to tell someone else. But this lack of information leaves you powerless to make changes and take action. Find the people in your life—personally or professionally—who will tell you the truth. Ask for feedback regularly from people you trust. Promise that no matter what people say, you will respond with "Thank you."

Make it easy for others to tell you the truth. The easier it is to give you feedback, the more information you'll get. The more information you have, the easier it is to manage your career, relationships, and results.

CHAPTER 13

DEALING WITH **DIFFICULT** SITUATIONS

Who needs reality TV when you have office drama? If you want to be entertained, just watch some of the crazy things people in your office do. Unfortunately, when you have to deal with these instances of crazy behavior, they're not so entertaining. People do things at work every day that make us want to lock ourselves in a conference room until everyone else has gone home. Coworkers give negative feedback in front of other people, break confidences they swore they'd keep, and linger in our offices for thirty minutes talking about nothing.

WHAT TO DO
WHEN YOU DON'T KNOW WHAT TO SAY

Time spent setting expectations and establishing working agreements definitely reduces the number of awkward conversations you will need to have. You'll know what people expect of you and vice versa. You won't have to guess what people need or what frustrates them. Missteps and mistakes will be reduced, but they won't be eliminated. Stuff happens. Unless you work alone all the time, you're not exempt from the craziness that ensues at work.

This chapter provides strategies for dealing with some of the most difficult situations that arise in the workplace. One note before we dive in: I wince every time I hear the term "dealing with difficult people." We deal with situations, not people. While some people may be difficult to work with and your world would get instantly better if they would go away, remember that no one wants to be "dealt with."

SITUATION: No matter what you do, one person remains difficult to work with.

Crazymakers are in every organization, everywhere. These are the people who deliberately stir things up and make things hard. They're the first people you are warned about when you join an organization—the ones whose presence at meetings evokes eye rolling and raised eyebrows.

Crazymaker is actually an academic term. If you take a college-level communications class, you will hear it. If you Google it, you will find numerous books written about these seemingly impossible people.

If you've tried everything within your power to work with someone, stop trying so hard. You can't work well with someone who doesn't want to work with you. But I do mean everything. Everything does not mean, *"I sent the person three emails and he didn't respond."* Or, *"I gave him feedback once and he didn't change his behavior. So now I have a pass to work around him."* Three emails and one conversation don't qualify as doing everything you can to get what you need from someone to create a good working relationship.

Everything includes several conversations and asking your boss or others to help broker the relationship. After you've done these things, be professional, courteous, and manage your emotions. If you can't get what you need to get your job done, ask someone to intervene who has a better relationship with that person.

I suspect many managers and organizational leaders would question me for suggesting you stop working on your most difficult working relationships. I'm not saying you should ignore the person or refuse to work with him. Instead, interact as well as you can and as much as you need to in order to do your job, but don't do more than that. Don't invest your time where you will not see a result. That's like trying to date someone who doesn't want to date you. We all know how that turns out.

SITUATION: You work for someone who doesn't provide enough feedback.

Managers are frequently promoted into management because they're good at their jobs. But doing something well and coaching someone else to do it are not the same thing. If all you hear from your boss is that you're doing a good job, and if you've tried the techniques for getting more feedback as outlined throughout this book and that hasn't worked, get feedback from a different source.

Don't sabotage yourself with the belief that your boss *should* give you feedback, and if he doesn't, it isn't your problem. Or by deciding that if there was negative feedback to give, someone would have told you. Until you hear otherwise, you'll just keep doing what you're doing. You already know people are not inclined to give feedback. No news is not necessarily good news.

If you do something poorly and don't get feedback, you still get a reputation for mediocre performance. People who are committed to their careers get the information they need, no matter what type of manager they work for. Anyone who sees you work may have insight into what you could be doing more effectively.

Simply ask your colleagues for specific feedback, and give coworkers permission to tell you. If the feedback isn't specific enough or you doubt its validity, ask someone else until you either get useful information or can validate the feedback you're questioning. While you deserve a boss who provides regular and specific feedback, you won't always have one.

SITUATION: You were promoted and now your former coworkers and friends work for you.

Managing people who were once your peers and are your friends is always awkward. How you handle the transition will determine how long the awkwardness lasts and how much authority and trust you earn with your new direct reports. Trust is earned, not awarded. You want employees who listen to you because they trust and respect you, not because of your title.

I suggest you practice something I call *name the game*, which is simply saying what you feel other people are thinking but will most likely not say. Just because your new direct reports don't tell you how much they wanted your job and how annoyed they are because they didn't get it, or how weird it is to be working for a friend, doesn't mean those feelings don't exist.

When you get promoted above coworkers and friends, I suggest having a one-on-one conversation with each new direct report and say, *"We were peers and friends, and now I'm your boss. It's awkward for me, and I have to assume it's awkward for you as well. I want us to have a good working relationship. The nature of our relationship will have to change. Before we go there, I want to give us both a chance to talk about how we're feeling. Want to start? What's this like for you?"*

These are obviously my words. Choose your own. But I recommend you have the conversation. The more transparent and willing you are to speak candidly about things people are thinking but not saying, the more respect you'll earn and the more solid your relationships will be.

SITUATION: You manage a team of people who were once your peers. You had the conversation described above with your new direct reports and talked openly about how uncomfortable it is to transition from being peers to a relationship in which you're the supervisor. But months later one of your employees still refuses to accept you as her

boss. She won't take direction from you and ignores your feedback.

This is a challenging situation. Use the Feedback Formula outlined in chapter ten to have a candid conversation.

STEP ONE: Open the conversation.

"I'd like to talk with you about our working relationship."

In this instance, skip step two.

STEP THREE: Share the behavior.

"Our relationship has been challenging since I started supervising the team. We've had a number of conversations about how much I'd like a good working relationship with you and about your resistance to accepting me as your supervisor."

STEP FOUR: State the impact of the behavior.

"The last time we talked I asked what you needed from me that you were not getting and what I could do to help you feel more comfortable with me as your supervisor. I don't know what else to do. Our relationship has not improved, and your resistance to my direction has become a performance issue. Either you need to accept me as the leader of this team or it's probably time for you to begin applying for other jobs."

STEP FIVE: Ask a question. Give the other person a chance to talk.

"What are your thoughts?"

STEP SIX: Make a suggestion or request.

"I'd really like to have you on the team, if you change your behavior. If not, let's figure out a transition plan for you."

You might be gasping, thinking there is no way you could ever have this conversation. It's definitely a tough message. This would not be your first, second, or even third conversation about this employee's resistance. While it's a difficult conversation, if you're in this situation and have the support of your boss and the human resources department, you will need to have it. Consider which is worse—having a short, challenging conversation or working with someone who treats you disrespectfully for months or even years.

SITUATION: You've given someone the same feedback repeatedly and nothing has changed.

When I do training and speak at conferences, the most frequent complaint I hear is, "I gave feedback, nothing changed, and there is nothing I can do." If you have given someone feedback and she hasn't changed her behavior, then she doesn't want to, can't, or doesn't know how to do what you're asking.

You need to determine why the person has not changed her behavior. If you decide she can do what you're asking and chooses not to, then the consequence of not changing is either nonexistent or not positive or negative enough to motivate behavior change. People change their behavior because of positive and negative consequences. No consequence, no behavior change.

If you feel you don't have the authority to hold someone accountable, I'd question that. You don't have to threaten someone's job, freeze her salary, or prevent her from applying for other roles to motivate different behavior. An effective consequence is addressing the behavior *every* time you see it—not every once in a while, but every single time. No one will enjoy being "talked to" every time she is late, misses a deadline, or wears inappropriate clothing. It's uncomfortable. It's also what we call being "managed out." Eventually, the person will get tired of these conversations and will either change her behavior or find another role, either within the organization or outside it.

SITUATION: You told someone something in confidence, and it came back to you from someone else.

When someone breaks your confidence, here's what you can do:

STEP ONE: Introduce the conversation. Explain what you're going to talk about and why.

> *"John, do you have a second? I wanted to talk with you about something I heard."*

In this instance, skip step two.

STEP THREE: Describe the observed behavior.

> *"I was talking to Sue the other day and she mentioned something that I had told you in confidence. That was between you and me. You gave me your word that you would keep it to yourself."*

STEP FOUR: Share the impact or result of the behavior.

> *"Hearing things I told you in confidence from other people makes me feel like I can't trust you."*

STEP FIVE: Have some dialogue. Ask the recipient for his perception of the situation.

> *"What happened?"*

STEP SIX: Make a suggestion or request for what you'd like the person to do next time.

> *"If I ask you to keep something to yourself, please do so. And if you feel like you can't, please tell me. If you do tell someone, please come tell me. I'd rather hear it from you than someone else."*

STEP SEVEN: Build an agreement on next steps.

> *"Are you willing to do that?"*

STEP EIGHT: Say "Thank you."

> *"Thanks for being willing to have this conversation with me. It was hard for me to talk to you about this. But our working relationship matters to me, and I want to feel I can trust you and continue to confide in you."*

SITUATION: Someone tells you about a problem but asks you not to say anything. Or someone gives you permission to pass the feedback on but doesn't want to be identified as the source of the information.

Being told something in confidence and then asked not to take action puts you in a very awkward position. When this happens, ask the person why he told you. Request that he not do it again unless he wants you to do something with the information.

There are times you simply cannot keep confidences. If this is the case, go back to the person who confided in you and tell her what you're going to do. Don't let her hear about it from someone else. The conversation could go something like this:

"Mary, I appreciate you telling me about the client's complaint. I know you asked me not to share it, and I want to respect your confidentiality. But it's a big deal and I have to pass on the feedback. How can I share the information so that you're comfortable? Do you want to talk to the director of sales yourself? I'm sure he'll be receptive. Or do you want me to talk to him?"

Here is another example: Let's say Sue told you something about John and wants you to take action but doesn't want to be identified as the source of the feedback. This too is challenging. The ideal thing to do in this situation is to help Sue plan a conversation with John. If Sue isn't comfortable having the conversation on her own, offer to help her lead the conversation. If she isn't willing to do either of these two things and you think it's important for John to get the feedback, you can deliver it yourself. But this is a last resort.

The conversation with John could go something like this: Give John the feedback. Then say, *"I can't identify the source of this information, and I know that's frustrating. Typically, if I can't share the source, I don't give the feedback. But I think it's important for you to know this.*

"Here is my suggestion, as difficult as this will be: rather than trying to figure out who said what, just alter your behavior. You might also tell the people with whom you work most closely that you got some feedback on

_____*and you're working to improve in that area. Tell your coworkers that you would appreciate any feedback they have. Then after you've made some changes, go back to them. Share what you've done differently and ask again for specific feedback."*

SITUATION: You applied for an internal job but didn't get it. You weren't given any feedback and you want to know why you didn't get the job.

Hiring managers are under no obligation to be candid with external candidates, but they do have a responsibility to help internal candidates grow and develop. Existing employees need and deserve candid feedback. That said, very few managers want to tell candidates why they didn't hire them.

The solution? Ask for the feedback. You may not get it, but you definitely won't if you don't ask. Tell the hiring manager, *"Thank you for the opportunity to interview. I'd really appreciate some feedback about what would have made me a better candidate. Anything you can tell me will be helpful."*

If you don't have access to the hiring manager, ask your boss for help. That could sound something like, *"Bob, I really appreciated the opportunity to interview for the marketing director role. I'd really like to get some feedback on what would have made me a better candidate. What's the best way for me to get that feedback? Would you be comfortable asking the hiring manager on my behalf?"*

SITUATION: Every time you give feedback to a certain person on your team, she cries.

Giving a crier feedback is uncomfortable. Some people say people cry to manipulate and get out of a situation. I don't think that's true. Rather, I think we all have a natural reaction to feedback and stress. Some of us clam up and say nothing, some of us get angry, and some of us cry. These are all natural reactions.

A person's response to feedback is not your problem. You're responsible for delivering feedback appropriately—behind a closed door, stating just the facts and focusing on behaviors and not emotion. But you are not responsible for how the recipient feels or reacts.

If she cries, hand her a tissue and keep talking. If the person is too emotional to participate in the conversation, end it. Say, *"I can see this is very upsetting and I'm sorry about that. Why don't we finish this conversation another time?"* When the person is calm, resume the conversation.

SITUATION: You attend a weekly meeting that is so unproductive, you can barely stand it.

Here is one of the most frequent complaints I hear from training participants: "All this candor stuff is nice, but if I don't lead the meeting there's not much I can do. I'm not in a position to tell the vice president, who is three levels above me, how to run his meetings."

Giving feedback to people above us, when we have no formal authority, is a challenge many of us know all too well. But there are a few things you can do. If you have a good relationship with the meeting facilitator, you can approach him and say something like, *"Running meetings of this size (or with this group) is really challenging. I wouldn't want to do it. I came across an article the other day that had some good ideas on how to run meetings like this one. Would you like me to make you a copy? Or would you like to hear a few of the ideas?"*

Or you could say, *"Running meetings of this size (or with this group) is really challenging. I wouldn't want to do it. I came across an article the other day that had some good ideas on how to run meetings like this one. It talked about having a back-up facilitator for when conversations get heated. Having a back-up facilitator allows the primary facilitator to step out and participate in the process, and it gives someone else the responsibility of managing the meeting during that conversation. The article also suggested giving difficult participants (like the people who speak too frequently or say no to everything) a job, like being the scribe. Would you like me to recommend any of these roles during the next meeting? I'm happy to help in any way that I can."*

Express some humility and offer to be helpful, rather than criticize the meeting facilitator, which will likely make him less accepting of your input.

If you feel you can't have this type of conversation with the meeting facilitator, find someone who can. It's likely that another person who attends the meeting has a close enough relationship with the facilitator that he can say something. Or consider who in the organization has the facilitator's ear and can have a conversation more comfortably than you can.

The conversation could go something like, *"Steve, I need to talk to you offline. I know you have a good relationship with Mike, and I was wondering if you could run a little interference. Mike's weekly meetings are really challenging. We talk about the same things repeatedly but never make any decisions. Would you be willing to talk to him about how he could improve the meeting? I don't think the message will be well received from me."*

Yes, my language here is pretty direct. Depending on whom you're speaking with, you may want to tone it down. For example, *"Steve, I need a little help. I've been attending Mike's weekly staff meetings. It's a tough meeting to run. There are several attendees with competing interests. Sometimes the meetings get out of hand. I want to help Mike, but I'm not sure how. You have a good relationship with him. What do you think about talking to him and making some suggestions, or asking if he'd like some help? I'd be happy to co-facilitate or help him add structure to the meeting."*

Everyone in an organization has someone he is close to and whom he confides in. That person can often say things that others can't. If you can find that person and he will protect your confidence while taking action on your behalf, that can be a very effective method of creating change.

SITUATION: One of your coworkers wants something from you and sends an email with a carbon copy (cc:) list longer than the guest list to your last holiday party.

People misuse the copy and reply-to-all functions on emails because they don't know it's inappropriate or because they don't think they will get what they need from you without alerting the whole world.

Someone may be using cc: as a wimpy way to alert your boss or colleagues that you don't make deadlines or meet your commitments. So she includes way too many people on emails hoping it will motivate you to act.

Copying everyone in an email can also be used to mean "I don't know why this email came to me. This is not my job," or "I need Joe's response before I can finish this project" (otherwise known as cover your butt). Again, email misuse could be simple ignorance (not stupidity, mind you; they're not the same thing), a case of not realizing that the whole world doesn't need the minute details.

If someone is inappropriately using cc: or reply-to-all and it bothers you, simply approach the person, state your observation, and ask a question.

STEP ONE: Introduce the conversation. Explain what you're going to talk about and why.

> *"Joan, do you have a second?"*

STEP TWO: If the conversation is not awkward or difficult, skip step two (empathize) and go directly to step three.

STEP THREE: Describe the observed behavior.

> *"I've noticed that when you need something from me you often copy the entire team in your email response."*

STEP FOUR: Describe the impact of the behavior.

> *"This is embarrassing and makes me feel you don't trust me."*

STEP FIVE: Have some dialogue. Ask the recipient for her perception of the situation.

> *"I'm wondering why you do that."*

If she says, *"The whole team needs that information. I'm just keeping people in the loop,"* you can reply with something like:

"I don't think the whole team needs to have that much detail. But let's add it as a topic to our next meeting agenda. We can talk about how much information people would like as projects progress and then make a decision as a team."

If instead she says, *"It's hard to get information from you. Sometimes I feel like the only way you get back to me is if other people are included on the message,"* you could use step six to form your reply.

STEP SIX: Request what you'd like the person to do next time.

"I'm sorry you feel that way. Would you be willing to speak to me directly the next time you request something and feel I haven't responded quickly enough? I'm very open to feedback, and I promise to be receptive."

This is an opportune time to use the Candor Questions provided in chapter three to talk about working-style preferences and setting expectations. You and Joan may have different definitions of what it means to respond in a timely way. For Joan, a timely response may be within two hours of receipt. For you, it may mean by the end of the week. Don't assume that you and Joan have the same preferences.

The conversation could go something like this:

"Joan, I'm realizing that when we started working together we never talked about our working-style preferences—our preferred method of communication, desired response time, how we will handle questions, and so forth. I think it would be really useful for us to have this conversation. What do you think? Would you like to do that now or schedule another time?"

SITUATION: Your boss tells you she is open to feedback, but when you give it, she gets defensive.

Giving anyone feedback is hard, but it's especially difficult to give it to your boss.

Feedback doesn't have to start with "*I disagree*," an opening that puts most people on the defensive. Asking a question can be an effective way to start to give feedback.

First say, *"The decision on _____ was really interesting."*

Then, when you want to share a counter point of view, ask one or two of the following questions.

▸ Can you walk me through how this decision was made? Or, what was the rationale for this decision?

▸ Where did this idea come from?

▸ I wonder what the outcome will be.

▸ One of our competitors did that last year. I wonder what kind of results they saw.

▸ What does Bob think of the idea?

No one likes to be told that she's wrong. There are lots of ways to disagree without actually saying you disagree. Open-ended questions open the door to a conversation when the questions are asked to genuinely understand something, rather than to accuse or make someone else appear wrong.

SITUATION: Your boss doesn't make time to meet with you. She cancels meetings. You can't move forward on projects without her input. As a result, your projects are running behind schedule.

Most managers are functional managers, which means that, in addition to managing people, they have their own accountabilities. Because they're so busy or may underestimate the importance of meeting individually with direct reports, many managers think team meetings or swinging by their employees' desks can replace traditional one-on-one meetings.

Conversations that occur naturally throughout the day do not replace scheduled one-on-one meetings. Every employee needs face time with his manager, whether he likes the manager or not. Short weekly or semi-monthly one-on-one meetings are ideal.

When it's hard to get time with your manager, tell her you know how busy she is and that you need her input to get things done. You'll also need permission to schedule meetings and to reschedule them when she cancels. Ask her assistant for help, if she has one. Her assistant will know the days when you're likely to be able to grab your boss for a few minutes and which appointments on her calendar are "real" or are blocked out for travel or focus time.

If you haven't already done so, ask your manager the best way to communicate with her—email or voicemail and office phone or cell. Ask if there is someone else who can sign off on work when she is unavailable. Suggest phone meetings during her daily commute or while she's traveling. Meetings don't need to be in person, nor do they need to be long. A lot can get done in fifteen minutes.

If none of these strategies work, consider moving forward with projects anyway. Use your boss's preferred communication method—email or voicemail—to send work-in-progress and status updates. Ask her to let you know if she wants you to do something differently.

SUMMARY: *YOU CAN SAY MORE THAN YOU THINK YOU CAN.*

Working with other people will always be challenging. When you get a group of people together who need to accomplish goals with limited resources and time, it's natural for conflict, power struggles, and territorialism to ensue. It's just the nature of working in an organization.

I encourage you to speak up and make requests. You can say more than you think you can, especially when your intention is to strengthen a relationship and improve results. If you wait too long to address an issue or say things you wish you hadn't, you can always clean it up.

Apologizing for how you managed something goes a long way and does not retract or invalidate your message. Suffering is optional. You'll feel better when you say what you need to say.

CHAPTER 14

BUSINESS RELATIONSHIPS THAT **REALLY WORK**

The foregoing thirteen chapters provided tools, language, and hopefully the inspiration you need to create the ideal place for you to work—an environment in which you don't have to guess what's important to people and in which you know the rules of the game and what you need to do to win.

In such an environment, when you make a mistake, someone tells you. Likewise, when you do something well and meet or exceed expectations, the people you work with are forthcoming with their feedback. Both positive and negative feedback is specific, clear, and useful. You always know where you stand with your boss, customers, and coworkers. You know your reputation and how others in the organization perceive you.

It's safe to ask questions and tell people, at all levels and in all roles, the truth. CEOs don't have to hire consultants to find out what's happening in the organization. Employees willingly tell them. Projects are completed smoothly, and teams and departments work well together because employees understand what other departments and individuals do and how they impact each other. More gets done, in less time.

When you know what others expect and what your coworkers think of your performance—because you asked—you're able to manage your reputation and thus your career. Information is power, and power means control.

Does this sound like an unrealistic, fantasy version of office utopia? Perhaps it is—today. But changing an organization's culture starts with one person who is willing to do something differently. One person who asks more questions and tells the truth. Is that you?

The difference between relationships that work and those that don't is courage—the courage to make requests and tell the truth. Likewise, one quality distinguishes people whose careers are on an upward trajectory from those who are in careers that stagnate. That, too, is courage.

You can say more than you think you can. Ask more. Assume less. Start today. You can do it!

ACKNOWLEDGMENTS

How to Say Anything to Anyone evolved from a fifteen-year career working in organizations where employees at all levels struggled to tell the truth at work. Here's a heartfelt "Thank you" to all the leaders, employees, colleagues, and customers with whom I've had the privilege to work, especially those who found the courage to say what they needed to say in the face of fear. Our work together and our many conversations created the true stories and examples that bring *How to Say Anything to Anyone* to life.

How to Say Anything to Anyone took three years to write and two years to edit. The book is indeed a labor of love, intended to save you, its readers, from the disappointment and frustration inherent in working with other people.

Specifically, thank you to Steven Shapiro for his endless patience in discussing how to best present this book. To Debra Fine, who encouraged me to keep going, when I wanted to quit. To Leslie Miller and Candace Sinclair, who helped shape the second and third drafts, and who always believed in me, my voice, and the book. And to Molly Moore for her brilliant cover design.

I hope *How to Say Anything to Anyone* gives you the language and courage you need to take control of your career and get more of what you want and less of what you don't at work.

ABOUT THE AUTHOR

Shari Harley started her career selling and facilitating programs for Dale Carnegie Training. She has also served as a trainer for American Century Investments, led leadership development and succession planning for OppenheimerFunds, and taught leadership courses at the University of Denver. She holds an MA in applied communication from the University of Denver and a BA in psychology from Washington University in St. Louis, Missouri.

In 2007 Harley left her corporate job to launch Candid Culture, a training and consulting firm that seeks to bring candor back to the workplace, creating a safe haven for employees and managers to speak honestly. Shari is known globally as an engaging, funny, content-rich business speaker, trainer, and consultant. Her practical approach to making business relationships work has enabled her to speak and train throughout the United States and in Singapore, Thailand, Malaysia, India, Dubai, and Australia.

Shari has a passion for international travel, and there are few places she won't go. When not traveling, speaking, or training, Shari spends as much time as possible outside. She lives in Denver, Colorado.

Learn more about Shari and Candid Culture's **training programs.**

Order *How to Say Anything to Anyone* for your organization.

leadershipandsalestraining.com

Get **TIPS** on how to be more candid on Twitter, Facebook, and YouTube.

 facebook.com/candidculture

youtube.com/shariharley

twitter.com/shariharley